GOD'S FAITHFULNESS
TO A COMMON *ORDINARY* PERSON

GOD'S PROVIDENTIAL CARE WORKING IN AND THROUGH MY LIFE

CAROL D HENRICH

TRILOGY

Trilogy Christian Publishers

A Wholly Owned Subsidiary of Trinity Broadcasting Network

2442 Michelle Drive

Tustin, CA 92780

Copyright © 2023 by Carol D. Henrich.

All Scripture quotations, unless otherwise noted, are taken from the Amplified® Bible (AMPC), Copyright © 1954, 1958, 1962, 1964, 1965, 1987 by The Lockman Foundation.

Scripture quotations marked kjv are taken from the King James Version of the Bible. Public domain.

All rights reserved, including the right to reproduce this book or portions thereof in any form whatsoever.

For information, address Trilogy Christian Publishing

Rights Department, 2442 Michelle Drive, Tustin, Ca 92780.

Trilogy Christian Publishing/ TBN and colophon are trademarks of Trinity Broadcasting Network.

For information about special discounts for bulk purchases, please contact Trilogy Christian Publishing.

Manufactured in the United States of America

Cover Design by: Jaimee Shaye

Trilogy Disclaimer: The views and content expressed in this book are those of the author and may not necessarily reflect the views and doctrine of Trilogy Christian Publishing or the Trinity Broadcasting Network.

10 9 8 7 6 5 4 3 2 1

Library of Congress Cataloging-in-Publication Data is available.

ISBN 979-8-88738-770-3

ISBN 979-8-88738-771-0 (ebook)

This book is dedicated to:

Holy Spirit,

the Spirit of Truth,

Who is my Helper, my Guide, my

Constant Companion!

My Love

However, I am telling you nothing but the truth when I say it is profitable (good, expedient, advantageous) for you that I go away. Because if I do not go away, the Comforter (Counselor, Helper, Advocate, Intercessor, Strengthener, Standby) will not come to you [into close fellowship with you]; but if I go away, I will send Him to you [to be in close fellowship with you]. John 16:7

Acknowledgments

I didn't tell anyone I was writing the book until I was essentially finished, which is why I'm not thanking people for helping me in regard to writing it.

But I do want to thank the following in relation to the book.

Many thanks to Terry Cordingley, my initial publisher contact at TBN/Trilogy, for his time and patience in answering all my upfront questions about this project. This is my first book, so my "C" type personality was flowing with a multitude of questions, and he was so kind and patient and graciously answered them all! Also want to thank Jennifer Hudson, my project manager, for her patience and help throughout the production process coordinating everything with the editing and design teams! I'm especially grateful for Lagene Gray's editing skills, and for the design team too. Thanks to Terry Cordingley for his help at the end of this publishing process too.

I want to thank a very special friend, Joyce Rickenbach, who has been a friend most of my entire Christian life—I'm so grateful for her friendship! She encouraged me when others didn't believe in me and during some tough times and continues to this day to encourage me in my walk with the Lord. Since telling her about the book, she has been a great encouragement and support to me regarding this as well!

So thankful to my daughter, Theresa P. Fackler, for her patience in teaching her momma how to do new things online, and especially relating to social media, which will help me reach many more people sharing about faith and trust in God through my book!

Contents

Preface   **1**

**Part One:
Life Without Jesus in It** **5**

Chapter 1
In the Beginning.. 7

Chapter 2
Growing Pains 11

Chapter 3
Looking for Love in All the Wrong Places 15

Chapter 4
Glimpses of God in My Life before Accepting Jesus 35

**Part Two:
Life With Jesus in It** **37**

Chapter 5
Being Born Again and Filled with Holy Spirit 39

Chapter 6
A Year of Praying and Trusting God to Meet Our Needs .. 55

Chapter 7
Living Word Training Center and Next Step 73

Chapter 8
God's Predetermined Places for Me to Live and Work
and His Providence Guiding Me to Them 87

Chapter 9
Divine Disruption on June 9, 2015 127

Chapter 10
Thoughts on Writing a Book 139

Chapter 11
A Quick Overview of My April 1 Experiences 143

Chapter 12
A Few Other Unique Experiences 151

Chapter 13
Disappointments 167

Chapter 14
BETH~EL: House of God, House of Prayer 173

Chapter 15
God Has a Plan for Each of Our Lives 181

Chapter 16
What Does the Future Hold? 189

Preface

Writing a book was never a dream, vision, or desire of mine; but Holy Spirit kept bringing it to my mind after over forty years of walking with Him, so I knew it was part of God's plan for my life. Writing about my life before the Lord was very difficult at times because I was not a good person and it was painful to recall things I had done, recall experiences, and be reminded of the person I was before asking Jesus to forgive my sins.

I shared a lot about my life before accepting Jesus so readers can understand the amazing transformation that took place after accepting Jesus. Holy Spirit changed me from the inside out and will continue His work until I'm called home to heaven.

Writing about my life after accepting Jesus was much easier; recalling things the Lord has done and experiences I've had with Him brings joyful memories to mind. Yes, there were difficult times too; but looking back, I can see that those times were all a part of God's plan of working all things together for good and getting me where He wanted me to be. Plus, they were times of growing in faith and trust and dependence on Him!

The two reasons for writing this book were:

First, to declare the works of the Lord and to praise and glorify Him for what He has done in and through my life and continues to do, and to pass this information on to the next generation.

I will praise You, O Lord, with my whole heart; I will show forth (recount and tell aloud) all Your marvelous works and wonderful deeds! Psalm 9:1

One generation shall laud Your works to another and shall declare Your mighty acts. Psalm 145:4

Second, to encourage others that God is faithful and worthy of our trust.

I will sing of the mercy and loving-kindness of the Lord forever; with my mouth will I

make known Your faithfulness from generation to generation. Psalm 89:1

Some personal names have been withheld to honor confidentiality.

My prayer is that your faith and trust in God will increase by reading about my life and that others will come to know Jesus because of reading it.

—Carol D. Henrich

Part One:

Life Without Jesus in It

Chapter 1

In the Beginning

My beginning was not like most childbirths per my Aunt Mae, the only living sibling out of nine children, when she told me the following: "Your mother thought she had to go to the bathroom, but you came into the world instead."

Due to my alcohol problem, which I'll go into in more detail later, I have very few memories of my growing-up years, and no memories of a happy, loving childhood.

I turned six in August 1950, and my mom died in December that year at the age of twenty-nine. I only remember seeing her three times.

First, Mom and I were on the back porch, and she was correcting me for something.

Second, Mom was lying in a bed with what appeared to me to be several medical people standing around the bed just looking at her.

Third, at Mom's funeral and all I could think about was, "What is wrong with me. Why can't I cry?"

My Aunt Mae also told me Mom lived like a vegetable for a long time, so it made sense that I would not have had a good relationship with her or have good memories. I have a couple photos of us, but that is about it.

My mom was born at home with the umbilical cord wrapped around her neck and her skin was blue. Naturally she lived, but then had heart problems all her short-lived life and was told she should never have children—I'm assuming that statement was made because they didn't expect her to live long enough to care for children!

I was told that she was very strict with my

brother and me, and found out decades later that her mom, my grandmother, was the disciplinarian of the family. I never heard of anything like what I'm going to share next: Aunt Mae told me that due to my mom's medical problems, when mom would do something wrong, Aunt Mae was the one who got disciplined! You heard that right, my aunt had to take the punishment when my mom did something wrong! I know Someone else Who did that too!

My dad, who had a twin that died in childbirth, had polio at a very young age and spent around ten years in a children's hospital in Philadelphia, Pennsylvania. He was crippled his whole life, one arm and the opposite leg, and never drove a car in his life. He was a watchmaker and worked at Hamilton Watch for many years, and repaired watches at home on the side. He loved taking pictures and had good camera and projector equipment. He also loved putting model trains together and was a part of the local model railroad club for as long as I can remember. He couldn't bowl due to being crippled, but he was picked up every week so he could get to the bowling alley where he tracked the scores for several bowling teams and then returned the following week with everything in order.

    Due to someone telling me that because my dad's polio went across his heart, he wouldn't be able to father children, I thought for years that he wasn't my father. I was told my mom wasn't faithful to my dad too, so again, was questioning who my father was. I have a boy's name, Dean, as my middle name and thought perhaps my real father was named Dean. Through a vision received while praying in 2020, when I was seventy-six years old, Holy Spirit revealed that the person I called my dad was indeed my dad. Don't know why I had to wait so long to find out, but so thankful that question in my heart has finally been settled!

Chapter 2

Growing Pains

Since my mom died shortly after I turned six years old, and my brother would have been close to eight years old, my dad had an aunt and another lady come to the apartment to care for us and clean for several years since he worked during the day. I don't know the number of years they helped us, but I do know I learned how to cook and clean at a young age and had a lot of responsibilities, along with my brother.

When we got a little older, my brother and I had a lot of freedom in our young lives, and I know we got in trouble too, but don't remember many details due to memory loss related to the alcohol problems. One thing I do remember is that we were dared to take some puffs on a cigarette, which we did, and when someone told our dad, we were punished for it.

We lived in a small apartment on the second floor that had three rooms and a bath. One room was a bedroom that my brother and I slept in, Dad slept on a chair or the couch in the living room, and naturally, there was a kitchen. There was also a porch off the kitchen and a large roof over the garage on the first floor we used. Our bath was a nice size, which also had a wringer washing machine and a big tub with two bins for rinsing clothes; yours truly did the wash and hung it on the porch and roof to dry.

Grocery shopping was one of my chores, probably by my teenage years. I had to walk to market and the grocery store and then carry the food and necessities back home in my arms, which were heavy at times. I didn't like doing it but had to do it anyhow.

Memories of being in school are few and far between.

Grade School: Fitted for my first pair of glasses.

Junior High: Was good at running in gym class—until I was in a race and fell, and no one encouraged me, so I stopped running.

High School: Learned typing and Gregg shorthand, and still use both to this day.

Recall using the pay phone at school to call the dentist since I was in so much pain in my mouth.

I had to stay after school to get help with algebra so I could pass the class.

Started a French-speaking class but dropped out almost immediately because I didn't like it.

Had a boyfriend during all of my high school years, which affected how much time was given to studying. I wasn't a bad student but wondered years later what would have happened if I would have applied myself in school.

I don't recall having a lot of new clothes growing up; wearing hand-me-downs is what I recall. Also, I don't remember shopping for clothes, again, the memory loss issue. But I do remember that I would go to department stores and steal clothes. I don't recall my dad ever questioning where I got the clothes from, either.

Encouragement and affirmation were something I don't recall receiving at home, or anywhere else for that matter, and never felt a sense of love and caring from my dad growing up. Years later, I came to realize he probably didn't know how to love and care for me emotionally and that his form of love was working to provide an income to provide a place to live and food to eat.

Chapter 3

Looking for Love in All the Wrong Places

As stated at the end of the last chapter, I never felt a sense of love and caring from my dad, so I started looking for love from men, or I should say boys, at around age twelve or thirteen. I had my first sexual relations with a boy at that age in my bed where I lived! I was shocked to see blood on the sheet and was quick to wash the bottom sheet to make it disappear before anyone saw it. I had no idea what happened to cause the blood at that time.

I continued looking for love, thinking I would find it through sex and had several boyfriends over the next couple of years and had a lot of sex, but not love! I didn't even know I was supposed to get anything out of sex until years later. I recall being asked if I got anything out of sex by a couple guys over the years, and I would lie and say yes! I also made a good housekeeper for a couple of guys, even though I wasn't living with them. Looking back, I would say I was more like an object than a girlfriend! I don't recall going out on dates like I know dates are supposed to be now; I would just be with someone and end up in bed, or cleaning. If I did go out on dates, the memory issue from alcohol wiped those memories away.

My one boyfriend had a motorcycle and road with the Sons of Satan club. At that time, I was proud to have my black leather jacket with the words "Sons of Satan" written on the back of it while riding the motorcycle. All I can say now is that God was so merciful to me and protected me through a lot at that time—even an attempted rape by one of his buddies while I waited outside in a vehicle when all the members were in the clubhouse at a meeting out in the woods. The guy was so much bigger and heavier than

I was, but I was able to fight him off, and then I just had to wait for my boyfriend when the meeting was over. He wasn't concerned about his buddy trying to rape me! I can't say for sure due to memory loss, but I'm assuming that is what brought about the end of our relationship.

Skydiving Adventure

I was bold, daring, courageous, fearless, and a risk taker in my late teens and early twenties, so when a guy I was seeing, Jay Harsh, and his friend, John Henrich, said they were going to skydive the following weekend, I said I wanted to do it too! They both came to my home and gave me instructions for two hours for the next four or five evenings, including how to land. I was jumping off steps practicing landings each night too. Also, I had additional training at the jump site prior to jumping.

Since I was under twenty-one years old at the time, I needed my dad's signature on a form giving me permission to do it. He wasn't in favor of it at first, but after a medical authorization was signed, my dad ended up giving his permission too. It's amazing what can happen in a week when one puts their mind to accomplishing something! This may have been the only time in my life that I knew my dad was proud of me because he talked to people about it and then was very disappointed when I told him I would no longer be jumping.

On Saturday, October 3, 1964, I made my first parachute jump at the Lancaster Airport in Pennsylvania with a lot of people watching. Since I was the first woman in Lancaster County to jump out of an airplane, the *Lancaster New Era*, a local newspaper, was there taking pictures and had a nice size write-up with pictures including a couple of me floating in the air under my chute in the October 6, 1964 edition of the paper! I still have the original article and pictures in a folder. Oh, back then all the jumps were solo since tandem jumps weren't invented until 1983. It was special to be a part of a team of five that started the Flying Dutchmen Sky Divers Club too.

Eventually I worked up to doing thirty second delays, being able to move around in the sky without being attached to anything before pulling the ripcord to open the parachute and I loved it! Various jumpers would get in formations holding on to one another at times, and guys loved being able to say they had midair kisses with me! One of my memorable experiences was falling through a big, white, puffy cloud on May 23, 1965—it was awesome! I had to keep watching my altimeter though, since I couldn't see the ground while inside of the cloud.

My dad never drove a vehicle in his life due to being crippled from polio at a very young age, so when Jay, John, and I went on a trip to an Air Force Base in the southern part of the country to visit one of our friends who was stationed there, that was when I learned to drive. Oh, I got a speeding ticket on the way back home—at midnight when no one was on the road except the cop! The cop was very nice and the record of it would not be transferred to Pennsylvania, so that was good, especially since I was on my learner's permit!

Women were not in the military back then, so the base was filled with all men, but the guys planned ahead and snuck me onto the base for a couple of days! A highlight of that adventure was going skydiving with a bunch of the guys from the base and giving some midair kisses so they could say they had a kiss in midair floating in the sky! I was happy to oblige them.

From October 1964 to June 1966, I logged a total of seventy jumps; also had a nine-month period in there where I didn't do any jumping—no, I wasn't pregnant! Just wasn't into it for a season. Perhaps I shouldn't have gone back to it at all, because my last five jumps weren't good ones, and my 70th one landed me in a tree—yes, I needed help to get down! My heart wasn't into it anymore! I still have my logbooks, though. Usually after a day of jumping was complete, a lot of people headed to the nearest bar to unwind, relax, and have fun. That wasn't a good habit for me to get into, and I'm sure it helped propel me into my drinking problem in the long run.

My First Marriage

John Henrich and I got married on November 22, 1965, and a couple of years later bought a home on Farmersville Road in Ephrata that was a new build in the process of being finished up. We had a beautiful daughter, Theresa Pauline Henrich, on May 19, 1968.

We had good times and not so good times in our marriage. A lot of what we did revolved around drinking in one way or another, which wasn't good for me. I was home for two years after having our daughter, was not happy, was drinking a lot, and started cheating on my husband with several men over the next couple of years, which I am not proud to admit, but it is the truth. He was a good man and didn't deserve that, but I couldn't help myself.

He didn't want a divorce even after he found out I was cheating on him, but I wasn't willing to keep trying and divorced him in 1973. This wasn't right either because he had the grounds to divorce me, not the other way around.

A few positive notes here: John remarried several years later, and we all ended up being good friends in the future and spent holidays and other times together. After I became a Christian, John and I talked about the past and I asked him to forgive me, which he did. I know he became a Christian a year or two before he died, so I am glad to know he is in heaven!

Scary Drinking Memories

Booze controlled me; I didn't control it. I couldn't have a couple of drinks and stop like most people did. Naturally, it didn't start out that way, but that's how it ended up. I had many long periods of blackouts where I'd be driving or doing things and not remember them. My guess is that half of my last year of drinking was spent in blackouts while drinking!

For some reason, the following memories are embedded in my mind and relate to blackout times I had during the last several years of my drinking. I'm not sure of the dates or the order in which they happened, so the following are not in chronological order.

◇ I know I was mad at my husband (or he could have been my ex-husband at the time), was drinking, and shouldn't have been on the road, but was driving late at night to go to good friends who lived in Manheim and got stopped by the police on the way there. I do recall he asked me where I was going, and I told him I was mad at my husband or something to that extent and was headed to my friends' home in Manheim. I have no idea why he let me go, as he could surely see I had too much to drink, but he let me go.

I'm pretty sure I got my friends out of bed. I'm not sure if the husband came and looked at my vehicle while I was still in the car or if I was inside with his wife at the time, but he ended up asking me what happened to the passenger side of my vehicle, which was a Ford LTD. I asked what he meant, and he said it was all crashed in on that side. I have no idea what happened, but was glad to be alive, and sad to say, but I'm sure I would have lied to the insurance company to get the repairs paid for by them.

◊ I was in a bar in a town called New Holland with a boyfriend and got mad at him about something. Getting angry and mean was a normal thing for me the last couple of years of my drinking. I drove my vehicle there, so I left and headed home. The next thing I knew, I went through a stop sign at the intersection of Route 322 and Railroad Avenue, hitting a log-type fence that was in front of a place selling cars. I immediately came to my senses! I got the name of the place and called them the next day. I think I sent a check to pay for repairs, but I'm not sure. I don't think there was much or any damage to my vehicle, even though I'm not sure how that would happen. That's all I remember except that I know this happened after my divorce. I have to say I believe God was watching over me, since I could have seriously injured or killed myself or someone else, since this was a very busy road normally! I don't recall having any injuries as a result of the accident.

  I went to the same bar the following night or a couple of days later, not sure which, and was told that I picked a fight with my boyfriend and was hitting him before I took off! I didn't remember that and still have no recollection of it. I was told by others in other situations that I would pick fights and hit people too.

  ◊ I have no idea when this happened, but I know I was at a bar in the country somewhere and think it was with my boyfriend, who became my husband eventually. I got angry and left and started walking on the country road next to a creek. The next thing I knew, I was in a vehicle with two guys at a red light at Manor and Charlotte Street in Lancaster, which was near my home. I got out of their vehicle and walked the rest of the way home. I have no idea what happened or how long it was from the time when I was walking on the country road to where I got out of their vehicle! I didn't have my purse, so I had to ring the doorbell to get into the apartment. My dad's girlfriend was visiting, and I heard her ask if I was okay, or something like that, and my dad answered, "She'll be okay."

    I know my dad was an alcoholic too. When I was younger, I used to wait up nights when he went out and watch for him to walk up the street beside the cemetery, which was across the street from where we lived. Once I knew he was safe, then I could go to sleep. One night he didn't come home for hours. I found out he was beaten and robbed, but I don't recall how he got home. As previously stated, he never owned or drove a vehicle due to being crippled in one arm and one leg.

◇ After the divorce and our home was sold, I used my share of the proceeds from the sale toward the purchase of a mobile home in Ephrata. It was a very nice and roomy 12' x 70' home. Two scary episodes relating to drinking I recall while living there were:

First, one morning when I went outside, I looked around and saw corn shucks all underneath the front of my vehicle, so I must have been out and about and in a cornfield somewhere the night before.

Second, I awoke one morning and went to the kitchen and saw the remainder of the eggs that I had made the night before on the stove, and a burner was still on! The silverware I used was inside the coffeepot on the stove, but on a different burner! Things I used to cook and eat were all over the countertop, along with six empty beer cans and a bottle of a fifth of whiskey over halfway empty! I was not a big beer drinker and much preferred whiskey but realized that I drank a six-pack of beer the night before too. That was very scary since that burner was left on all night.

I believe the second episode mentioned above was what led me to call the pastor of a Mennonite Church I attended several times in a town called Akron. I must say I had never felt love before like I did the times I visited that church, and I know they could tell I either had been drinking or was hungover from the night before! I still occasionally think of those times I visited and the love I felt! Back to the call to the pastor: he agreed to visit me, and I had been drinking when he came, but he stayed and talked with me for what seemed like a couple of hours. I know I really appreciated his time sharing with me and praying for me.

I had been showing up for work late almost every day with bloodshot eyes, and I was meeting with people looking to purchase personal lines insurance, so bloodshot eyes were not easy to hide since I couldn't wear sunglasses at work. Yes, I had my whiskey at work too, but to my knowledge, no one knew it. Several people had been encouraging me to go to Alcoholics Anonymous (AA) meetings, including my ex-husband and my employer for quite a while, but I would respond that I didn't have a problem and didn't need to go to AA.

    I believe it was days, or maybe weeks, after the pastor I mentioned above came to visit me that I was so down one night that I cried out to God for help. I ended up at an AA meeting the next day, which was April 1, 1974. I mention the exact date because some great things have happened to me over the years on an April 1, so I always look forward to that date! I'm sorry to say I did drink after the AA meeting, but I went back the next night and continued going to meetings two nights a week for months and then went down to one night for several more months. My ex-husband was a big help with watching our daughter when I went to meetings, as well as other people who helped too. Those meetings were a lifeline to me at the time, enabling me to stay sober. I heard that some people were saying I wasn't taking care of my daughter with all the meetings I was attending, but they didn't understand that I needed to take care of myself before I could take care of her. My ex-husband had no problem with me attending a lot of meetings and was glad I was because he knew I needed help!

I was sober for about two years when I wanted to see if I could drink again, so I asked my ex-husband if I could go out drinking with him and the others and he said yes. He even planned for someone to watch our daughter. Well, I got drunk and mean and ugly just like I did in the past, so I stopped drinking again!

A Second Marriage—But Not Really

One of the places I attended AA meetings was at The Gate House in Lititz, Pennsylvania. I was attracted to a man who was living there and was in rehab, and he was attracted to me as well. We started seeing each other and the next thing I knew, we were talking about living together. I invited him to come live with me and my daughter, which he did. It didn't take long to discover that this was a wrong move. I had a job, and he didn't; he did receive disability payments from the government from being in the service. He just slept most of the day while I was working, which was frustrating to me.

After a while, he advised me that his ex-wife didn't want their two children, and we talked about them coming to live with us, as my heart went out to them. I couldn't understand a mother not wanting her children. My thoughts were that if we were to get married and his children would come to live with us, then hopefully he would change and become the husband and father he should have been. We did get married in August 1975 by someone he knew. This person was telling us who we were in a past life, which at the time didn't set alarms off inside me since I wasn't a Christian then. His children came to live with us, but it ended up that I had four children to care for because he didn't change, except he got worse, and was just like a child. He was asleep in bed when I went to work in the morning, and he was on the couch sleeping when I got home from work in the afternoon.

He didn't have any credit, so soon after we were married, I signed my vehicle and mobile home over to him so he could establish credit! When you think you are in love and believe everything someone tells you, a person does some very stupid things, and this was a big one for me!

In December 1975, my ex-husband called late one night and advised me that his dad had passed away, and he wanted to let me know. I was naturally sorry to hear that, but it also got me thinking about life and the life I was currently living. On January 1, 1976, I decided that I wasn't going to spend the rest of my life living like I was, that I was stronger than my current husband, and that I would get out of this marriage and set my mind to do so. I felt bad for all the children because my daughter finally had the siblings she always wanted, and the three of them got along most of the time, but now, somehow, that was going to end.

The next year wasn't easy. I discovered he was drinking again, which the children knew as well. His children went back to live with their mom after the school year ended, and I worked on getting my vehicle and mobile home back into my name, which I did. He moved out in August 1976. I agreed that he would divorce me instead of me divorcing him.

It wasn't finalized until October 1977. I didn't care about that, I just wanted out of the marriage and to get on with life.

Let me fast forward a little here to insert some future details that make sense to share at this point. I'm not sure of the exact timing, but believe it would have had to be in 1980 that I received a call from the mom of my stepchildren advising me they were all in Ohio and wanted to return to Pennsylvania but didn't have a place to stay. I invited them to come live with my daughter and me in our apartment, which they did. During the several months they were with us, I learned that almost everything our ex-husband ever told me was a lie! She would just be sharing things and I'd think to myself, that's not what he told me, and shared what he told me with her too. One of the major things she shared was that she told our ex-husband that she felt their children would be better off with both a father and mother role models in the home rather than just a single mom and had asked about them living with us. Wow, what an eye opener, but was so glad to learn it wasn't that she didn't want them! I trusted him and shared so much with him, but after learning that he was a habitual liar, I had a hard time trusting anyone— especially men!

Another Bad Decision

I sold the mobile home, and my daughter and I moved into a second-floor apartment up on Main Street not far from where we had been living. I started seeing a guy who moved in with us. I'm not sure how long he lived with us, but I wasn't happy and told him he needed to leave. He did leave, but one day he ended up on the roof overhang, trying to get in, and he had a rifle with him! I kept telling him to get down and leave and that if he didn't, I was going to call the police. He eventually got down, but then sat in the parking area out back with a gun pointed at his head. I yelled down that he needed to leave or I was calling the police, and he did leave. That was a scary time. Thankfully, my daughter didn't experience that too.

I wish so many things would have been different for my daughter's childhood and memories, but she turned out great in spite of me! I can't change the past, but it is forgiven!

Chapter 4

Glimpses of God in My Life before Accepting Jesus

◊ I was in the hospital for a third operation to have cysts removed from my ovaries. A pastor's wife of a friend visited me in the hospital and prayed for me. She also gave me a book by Oral Roberts called *Daily Guide to Miracles*.[1] I was expecting a lot of pain due to my experiences with the previous two surgeries, but I had NONE! Even though I had no pain, the doctor and nurses still wanted me to take pain meds, but I said I had no pain and wouldn't take them. Somehow, I knew the prayers of the pastor's wife were effective, resulting in no pain this time!

◇ Prior to accepting Jesus, God sent a pastor looking for insurance to where I was working. I don't recall if he purchased insurance, but I do know that he shared God's love with me and encouraged me to seek Him. I know the seeds he planted that day influenced my life.

◇ I started having rough times late at night when my daughter was at her daddy's for the weekend and would think of suicide. When this happened, I would go inside the Lutheran Church in Akron and sit down. I would just sit there for a while and felt a peace and calm when I left, so I knew something was special there. Sometimes I would go there on lunch breaks too, since I worked close by, and I experienced that same peace and calm when I left. Thankfully, back at that time it was open to the public twenty-four hours a day and seven days a week, so I could go there late at night and get inside. There was a Lutheran Church right across the street from where I lived, but it wasn't open all hours of the day.

Part Two:

Life With Jesus in It

Chapter 5

Being Born Again and Filled with Holy Spirit

As mentioned in Part One of this book, I was looking for love through sex and figured when I found the man who would satisfy me through sexual intercourse, then I would have found love! I know it was such wrong thinking, but living without Jesus, the enemy controls our thoughts. Finally, when I was thirty-four, I found the first guy who ever satisfied me in bed, but there was only one problem—he loved the barmaid who worked down the street and was just seeing me on the side, so to speak. I knew it wasn't going to work for us to be together, so from somewhere deep inside, thoughts came back to me from the *Oral Roberts Daily Guide to Miracles* book. The thoughts were about giving up something out of my need, knowing God would give me back something better, and that's what I did. I gave him up and over to God, knowing He would give me back something better, and I ended up receiving the best possible thing in return—Love Himself, Jesus!

I have wondered in the last couple of years if God prohibited me from enjoying sex, kind of like when he closed the wombs of women in the Bible until it was the perfect time in His plan for them to have a child, and I truly believe He did.

On March 28, 1979, starting at 4:00 a.m., the Three Mile Island Nuclear Power Plant in Middletown, Pennsylvania began a partial meltdown of the Unit 2 reactor, which was the most significant accident in U.S. commercial nuclear power plant history. On the seven-point International Nuclear Event Scale, it was rated Level 5—Accident with Wider Consequences.

Three Mile Island was less than an hour away from where my daughter and I were living in Ephrata.

My ex-husband, John, was high up in PPL's union at the time and, therefore, had some inside information regarding the accident. He said it didn't look good. He advised me to pack up some things for my daughter and me and come to his home in Lancaster. He said we would all go to Delaware to one of his relative's homes to get farther away from the accident site. I wasn't afraid due to the accident, but my daughter was also his daughter, so I honored what he said and packed some things in the car and went to his home in Lancaster. Upon arriving at his place, he advised me to put the things I brought in his car and truck, and we would all ride together.

After we were on the road a short time, all I could think about was **what am I going to do if I can't go back since I don't have my car?** I didn't want to be dependent on my ex-husband, his mom, or any of his relatives. My mind was filled with that thought, and it kept playing over and over and over in my mind and literally consumed me. We were very near the ocean, and I could hear the waves on the beach, which didn't calm me down inside. There wasn't much, if any, sleep that first night. The second night, lying in bed, thoughts from the book called *Daily Guide to Miracles* came back to me that God is my Source, and I don't need to be concerned about being dependent on others! I believed that statement in my heart, gave the whole thing over to God, and had a good night's sleep the second night.

The very next day, John advised me that another woman who drove separately from Lancaster to Delaware was going back to Lancaster, and she said I could return with her if I wanted to. John then advised I couldn't take my daughter along, though. I knew she would be safe with him, so I returned without her.

The evening that I returned home, I went to visit a friend who lived a couple of blocks away from me and had been witnessing to me about the Lord. I stayed a couple of hours and then very close to midnight I was going to walk home, which wasn't a problem back in those days, but she insisted on driving me. Prior to getting out of her car, she asked if she could pray for me. I said yes, thanking her after she prayed, and then got out of her car and went upstairs to my apartment. Shortly after midnight on April 1, 1979, I got down on my knees beside my bed and invited Jesus to come into my life and to forgive me for my sins!

WOW, I cannot explain the changes that happened in my life from the inside out, except to reference 2 Corinthians 5:17, **"Therefore if any person is [ingrafted] in Christ (the Messiah) he is a new creation (a new creature altogether); the old [previous moral and spiritual condition] has passed away. Behold, the fresh and new has come!"** This is exactly what happened in me, for the old self just wasn't there any longer. Immediate major changes included:

◇ Unable to swear anymore—I had a very foul mouth before accepting Jesus and the "F" word came out of my mouth all the time. I can't stand to hear people say the "F" word now. It hurts on the inside, especially when I hear Christians saying it because they are not respecting and honoring God by using it! To me, Christians saying the "F" word are belittling themselves, and certainly don't know what God's Word says about the words we speak. I pray they come to know the truth of Ephesians 4:29:

Let no foul or polluting language, nor evil word nor unwholesome or worthless talk [ever] come out of your mouth, but only such [speech] as is good and beneficial to the spiritual progress of others, as is fitting to the need and the occasion, that it may be a blessing and give grace (God's favor) to those who hear it.

The foul and polluting language was no longer a part of my life, but I cannot say that I've never had any worthless talk ever come out of my mouth. The Christian walk is a daily work in progress, and we are being changed as we renew our minds in the Word of God.

◊ The desire for men and for sex left me, except when an old boyfriend who had lived with me for a time visited and wanted back into my life very soon after I became a Christian. I ended up having sex with him on the kitchen floor, but afterward my heart was so heavy and hurting. I cried and cried and was so very sorry I did it and hurt Jesus! I received forgiveness and moved forward.

◊ I used to make fun of people and laugh at them, but that was no longer a part of the new person I was in Christ.

◊ I never liked to read in the past, but now I had a great hunger for the Word and was in it as much as possible, learning about the Man Who truly loved me and gave His life for me so that I could be forgiven and be born again and could find out who I was in Christ.

I felt more love coming from my relationship with the Lord and the Word than I ever felt with a man, and that's because I was now experiencing true love, and no man without Christ has true love! God is LOVE!

◊ I'm not sure when it happened but I could no longer call myself an alcoholic because I was now a new creation in Christ, was set free from that bondage, and I knew my heavenly Father would not call me an alcoholic!

◇ I smoked non-filter Camel cigarettes for many years and had no desire to quit when I first became a Christian, even though my daughter and others were encouraging me to do so. But then about eight months or so into my Christian walk, Holy Spirit let me know it was time to quit by taking me to Romans 8:13, **"For if ye live after the flesh, ye shall die: but if ye through the Spirit do mortify the deeds of the body, ye shall live"** (KJV).

I tried and tried on my own strength and changed to filtered cigarettes, which I didn't like, but it wasn't working, and I was feeling guilty for not being able to do it. Then Holy Spirit directed me to use my faith by applying the following two Scriptures:

And this is the confidence that we have in him, that, if we ask anything according to his will, he heareth us: And if we know that he hear us, whatsoever we ask, we know that we have the petitions that we desired of him. 1 John 5:14–15 (KJV)

As it is written, I have made you the father of many nations. [He was appointed our

father] in the sight of God in Whom he believed, Who gives life to the dead and speaks of the nonexistent things that [He has foretold and promised] as if they [already] existed. Romans 4:17

So I prayed one last time, asking God to enable me to quit smoking, knowing this was in accordance with His will for me and, therefore, He heard me. From that time on, I spoke as if I had already quit smoking, even though in the natural I was still smoking. I was calling those things that be not as though they were, like God did with Abraham, calling him the father of many nations before he ever had a son. Every time I lit up a cigarette, regardless of where I was, I would say, "Thank You, Father, that I quit smoking!" People would look at me and say, "You are lying," but then I would tell them I was using my faith and share the two Scriptures with those who would listen. I know it was several weeks, or could have been a couple of months, that I did this without any feeling of guilt. Then Holy Spirit directed me to Exodus 33:14, **"And the Lord said, My Presence shall go with you, and I will give you rest."** From that time on, for several days, I had such a strong presence of the Lord that I never even thought about lighting up a cigarette; then as the week went by, His presence diminished little by little each day. I have never had, or desired, a cigarette from that time on, can't stand to smell it when around people who are smoking, and do my best to stay away from where people are smoking.

I have applied these Scriptures in other situations with successful outcomes too and have shared them with many others who were struggling to overcome things in their lives.

I changed in so many ways from the inside out. Without Jesus in my life, I was being controlled by the flesh and the devil, but now I was a new creation. The easiest way to explain what happened is to share the following Scriptures:

I have been crucified with Christ [in Him I have shared His crucifixion]; it is no longer I who live, but Christ (the Messiah) lives in me; and the life I now live in the body I live by faith in (by adherence to and reliance on and

complete trust in) the Son of God, Who loved me and gave Himself up for me. Galatians 2:20

And you [He made alive], when you were dead (slain) by [your] trespasses and sins In which at one time you walked [habitually]. You were following the course and fashion of this world [were under the sway of the tendency of this present age], following the prince of the power of the air. [You were obedient to and under the control of] the [demon] spirit that still constantly works in the sons of disobedience [the careless, the rebellious, and the unbelieving, who go against the purposes of God].

Among these we as well as you once lived and conducted ourselves in the passions of our flesh [our behavior governed by our corrupt and sensual nature], obeying the impulses of the flesh and the thoughts of the mind [our cravings dictated by our senses and our dark imaginings]. We were then by nature children of [God's] wrath and heirs of [His] indignation, like the rest of mankind.

But God—so rich is He in His mercy! Because of and in order to satisfy the great and wonderful and intense love with which He loved us,

Even when we were dead (slain) by [our own] shortcomings and trespasses, He made us alive together in fellowship and in union with Christ; [He gave us the very life of Christ Himself, the same new life with which He quickened Him, for] it is by grace (His favor and mercy which you did not deserve) that you are saved (delivered from judgment and made partakers of Christ's salvation).

And He raised us up together with Him and made us sit down together [giving us joint seating with Him] in the heavenly sphere [by virtue of our being] in Christ Jesus (the Messiah, the Anointed One).

He did this that He might clearly demonstrate through the ages to come the immeasurable (limitless, surpassing) riches of His free grace (His unmerited favor) in [His] kindness and goodness of heart toward us in Christ Jesus.

For it is by free grace (God's unmerited favor) that you are saved (delivered from judgment and made partakers of Christ's salvation) through [your] faith. And this [salvation] is not of yourselves [of your own doing, it came not through your own striving], but it is the gift of God;

Not because of works [not the fulfillment of the Law's demands], lest any man should boast. [It is not the result of what anyone can possibly do, so no one can pride himself in it or take glory to himself.]

For we are God's [own] handiwork (His workmanship), recreated in Christ Jesus, [born anew] that we may do those good works which God predestined (planned beforehand) for us [taking paths which He prepared ahead of time], that we should walk in them [living the good

life which He prearranged and made ready for us to live]. Ephesians 2:1-10

I was a new creation and really liked the new me, but my life changed so drastically that most of my friends and acquaintances who were unbelievers had a hard time accepting the changes in me, which resulted in people rejecting me, talking and sneering behind my back and in front of me.

I am in awe and wonder of the supernatural rebirth that took place in me!

Something Special from God for Me

The night I was born again, I was drawn to look out my bedroom window, and to my amazement, the stained glass windows in the Lutheran Church across the street were lit up and full of beautiful colors! They were never lit before at night, and I knew inside it was God doing something special just for me. They continued being lit every night until I went to visit The Worship Center church that was meeting in Lititz, Pennsylvania at the time, where I received the baptism of the Holy Spirit and immediately started speaking in tongues. I ended up lying on the floor and tongues kept flowing forth from me for a very long time. When I looked out my bedroom window that night, the stained glass windows were not lit up and were never lit up again! I don't know if God had someone turning them on just for me, or if I was the only person seeing them lit up, but either way, it was a special sign from God for me.

Naturally, I didn't understand all that was happening to me, but I found myself praying in tongues all the time, and I truly believe a part of that was to build myself up praying in tongues, or in the Holy Spirit, as it states in Jude 20, **"building up yourselves up on your most holy faith, praying in the Holy Spirit"** (KJV). This was to help me deal with the persecution and rejection I was receiving because my life had changed so drastically. I knew inside that praying in tongues would be a big part of my Christian life. For this, and other reasons, I remain thankful that I didn't grow up in a church filled with traditions, but am able with simple childlike faith to trust God and His Word.

No Question About It, I Became a Fanatic

After accepting Jesus and after all the changes happened in my life, I would talk to anyone and everyone about Jesus—in a store or on the street, anywhere! I used to walk up to people and ask to pray for them if they had a physical problem. It didn't matter to me what anyone thought of me or how they responded to me; I just wanted to share and to help people.

I also used to drive some people, including family members, crazy with all my talk about Jesus, but I couldn't **not** share about my new life and excitement about Jesus!

Chapter 6

A Year of Praying and Trusting God to Meet Our Needs

I was still a baby in the Lord, learning how to hear and follow His voice and promptings in my spirit when the thought of quitting my job so I could be home praying and trusting God for everything kept getting stronger and stronger within me! I didn't know of anyone who could relate to what I was experiencing on the inside to talk to about it, and people I shared this with didn't believe God was asking me to do it. I knew my calling was prayer, so what was on my heart made sense to me, and thankfully the following Scriptures were, and continue to be, so important to me:

Lean on, trust in, and be confident in the Lord with all your heart and mind and do not rely on your own insight or understanding. In all your ways know, recognize, and acknowledge Him, and He will direct and make straight and plain your paths. Proverbs 3:5-6

Roll your works upon the Lord [commit and trust them wholly to Him; He will cause your thoughts to become agreeable to His will, and] so shall your plans be established and succeed. Proverbs 16:3

My daughter was only twelve when these thoughts wouldn't leave me, and Holy Spirit was giving me more faith to step out in faith and be obedient. I talked to my daughter's father about this, and I was so surprised that he wasn't against it! We were divorced, and he gave me $100 a month toward her care, which would be the only definite income I would have. His agreement gave me a boost of confidence to move forward.

Well, I came up with a different plan than

God's and had a meeting with the owner of the company I was working for, who was a Christian. I shared what God had put on my heart and asked if I could work half days and spend the other half at home with the Lord in prayer, and he agreed. WOW! I was so happy and looked forward to what God had planned!

The very next day after the owner gave me permission to work half days, the office manager came to me and said I had a decision to make: either I stop talking about Jesus, period, when in the office—or I could quit. He never liked it that I would talk to people about Jesus and hand out little booklets about Him to people who came into my office for personal lines insurance quotes and policies. He liked the old Carol before Christ came into my life but never accepted the new, born-again Carol, since my life changed so drastically! Most people didn't accept the new me, so I was learning to deal with persecution early on in my Christian life.

What did I do with the ultimatum given to me? I said, "I quit," gathered all my personal belongings, immediately walked out, and never regretted it! I never talked to the owner about it because I knew inside this was God's way of directing my steps to walk in obedience to His plan to leave my job and be home praying and trusting in Him to meet our needs—He didn't say half days! Someone hinted to me later that the office manager went to the owner and said either I go or she goes. This was all a part of God's plan to get me where I was supposed to be! This reminded me of Abraham and Sarah coming up with their own plan to fulfill the promise God spoke to them, but God doesn't have a Plan B! This would not be the only time God called me to do something out of the ordinary that people didn't believe was God's Plan!

So What Do I Do Now?

So what do I do now? I do what God told me to do—PRAY—and read the Word and trust Holy Spirit to direct me what to do from day to day.

My life went from living a normal day-to-day routine to not having a routine, which was very strange for me, except that taking care of my daughter was the only constant as far as any routine.

I was already praying in tongues a lot, so when God called me home to pray it was a natural thing for me to spend hours praying in tongues, and at times praying in English as Holy Spirit led, but English did not always follow tongues. I know I spoke in tongues more than English during this year at home, and I continue to speak in tongues often and for long periods of time, depending on the guidance of Holy Spirit. It is just a huge part of my Christian life and I am so thankful God blessed me with this gift!

I prayed in tongues so much during that year that I identified with what Paul said in 1 Corinthians 14:18, **"I thank God that I speak in [strange] tongues (languages) more than any of you or all of you put together."** In 1 Corinthians 14, Paul is also talking about the gift of tongues and interpretation in a church service and says in vs. 28, **"But if there is no one to do the interpreting, let each of them keep still in church and talk to himself and to God."** This Scripture states speaking in tongues is a way to talk to God and to themselves!

During my year at home praying, Holy Spirit

guided me to pray for a lot of different circumstances, people, and countries, but I wasn't journaling at that time; I wish I would have now, but had no idea God would call me to write a book 40+ years later. We need to submit ourselves to Him in prayer, ask what He wants us to pray about, take the time to listen, and then pray according to what Holy Spirit puts on our hearts. I did a lot of this type of praying while at home that year. Yes, we pray about things we are aware of in the natural and things people have requested prayer for, but God has things on His heart He wants prayed about too, and we need to ask Him what they are!

I now know that all the time praying in tongues the first two years of my Christian life was also building me up for that year at home, as well as for things that would happen during my Christian walk as my faith and trust in God grew exponentially early in my walk with the Lord!

A Couple Special Prayer Times During That Year I Will Never Forget

First: My daughter and I used to spend time

praying in tongues together daily. One day she came out very strong and rebuked a fire. She was used to hearing me rebuking things, but this was new for her to do it. When we finished our prayer time, she got up and started walking away, but I stopped her and asked if the Lord showed her something regarding a fire. Here is what she shared:

She said my bed was on fire, and I was on it and was dead! Then she continued walking into the kitchen! WOW!

I was shocked and amazed at the same time, but I knew immediately what I needed to do. There was a defective light connected to the top of my bed that I used for reading, so I went and took it off my bed and put it in the trash! My daughter saved my life! A quick note here—years into the future, my daughter's daughter saved her life as well—more on that later in the book.

Second: A couple at my church were going on a mission trip for a couple of weeks to a country in Central America. I knew inside I was supposed to be praying for them, and I told them I would. One day while sitting in my chair and praying in tongues for them, suddenly I was in the spirit and in the same location where they were; it was like a jungle setting. I saw the husband outside doing something and was communicating with him, not verbally, but spirit to spirit. I didn't see his wife, so I asked him where she was, and he said she was inside—the word "hut," comes to mind for what she was in—and he advised me she was bleeding! This was not good since she was pregnant! Then again, suddenly, I was back in my chair and praying for her and took authority over the bleeding and commanded it to stop. This experience made me think this must be what it's like communicating with each other in heaven.

    Naturally, I was amazed, but also questioned inside what had just happened, and it was on my mind every day. I knew I had to go and see the woman after they got back home and tell her what had happened and see how she would respond. I was nervous but did go to the church, saw her, and told her exactly what I experienced. She confirmed that she was bleeding while they were away! I am happy to report that she gave birth to a healthy child at her appointed time!

All I can say is, what an amazing experience to see what our Father will do to help His children! Naturally, a lot of praising and thanksgiving was given to Him as well!

Some of God's Provisions

I wish I could say that I was a mighty woman of faith during that whole year, but I wasn't, as I carried the concern of where the money would come from for the first several months. Then, while in prayer one day, Holy Spirit spoke and said,

**"Fret not for your finances, for
I will prosper them."**

I didn't even know the word fret was in the Bible, but I looked and there are several places that say "fret not!" I received that word and from then on didn't have any care about how or what the Lord would provide; I just knew He would!

A neighbor behind us had a garden and gave us a lot of food, even though she didn't believe in the beginning that God had called me to do this, and others provided food and meals for us too. At times, people would invite us to lunch after church, which was a blessing. My brother, who prefers to remain anonymous, was a huge blessing to us as well, since he owned a produce business. I was helping him on Saturdays at market, and I could take whatever produce I wanted; he also paid me for working! He loves giving and has blessed an untold number of people over the years in many ways!

I'm not sure when it started, but an interesting phenomenon started happening prior to when someone was going to give me money:

One or both of my ears would get bright red and burn!

This became a normal occurrence prior to when someone was going to give me money, so when it happened, I expected it. I wasn't surprised when someone blessed us but was still very thankful and appreciative for every gift! I don't know why God did this, but He did it, and I will never forget those unique experiences! Hindsight leads me to think these experiences probably started after He told me not to fret about finances and that he would prosper me, but I don't know that for sure.

There were times when I didn't even have one dollar for gas. The idea came to mind to talk to the owner of the gas station where I got my gas to ask him to donate the gas I needed—that was a very bold move for me—and I would in turn be praying and believing that God would prosper his business, which was not doing well at the time. He didn't agree, which I totally understood since he really didn't know me except for getting my gas there. He did end up going out of business. Lord only knows if things could have been different.

Some Other Sources of Income the Lord Provided

1. Holy Spirit put it on my heart to sell some things that weren't being used to generate some money, which I was very agreeable to do.

2. When the school at my church needed a van driver to pick up children to take to school and then back home again, I was approached about that and sensed I should help for a while, so I agreed and

that generated a little income too. That was a fun experience with the children, even in the snow on the back country roads!

3. I also taught an evening class on prayer at my church and an offering was given at the end of that class.

Once while reading the Word, Philippians 4:6, really stuck out to me; it says:

Do not fret or have any anxiety about anything, but in every circumstance and in everything, by prayer and petition (definite requests), with thanksgiving, continue to make your wants known to God.

That Scripture was not new to me, but this time it was very strong inside of me that I needed to be very specific when asking God for what I needed and be thankful for the answer at the same time. The following are two answers to prayer that I will never forget, and a blessing I didn't even request:

◊ One month I had a need for $500, which included my annual car insurance, which was a lot cheaper back in the early '80s. I presented my need to God, advising the amount that was needed and what it was needed for, and then continued throughout the month thanking Him for it.

A Larry Burkett Financial Meeting was scheduled to be held at our church. I was praying for the meeting and was able to attend without paying a registration fee. At one point during the seminar, the speaker was sharing on 2 Thessalonians 3:10, which says at the end, **"If anyone will not work, neither let him eat."** I was in the front row and wanted to sink in my chair, as I felt like everyone was looking at me since a lot of people knew I wasn't working! Then, during a break, the pastor of the church came to me and said he wanted to talk to me after the meeting was over. Well, the thoughts that were going through my mind until the end of the meeting were negative things like, **what did I do wrong,** instead of any positive thoughts.

When the meeting was over, I went to the pastor, and he shared that someone gave an anonymous gift for me in the amount of $500 and a check would be sent to me! I could not contain myself and praised and thanked the Lord over and over and said many Hallelujahs! I asked, but naturally the pastor wouldn't tell me who gave the gift so that I could thank them personally, but I just know they saw my excitement and the thankfulness that was given to God because of their giving! After the Lord put me back to work, I loved giving anonymous gifts to people I didn't know who were in need as Holy Spirit led me to do.

◇ Another time, there was a need for a specific amount. I don't recall the amount but know it was not an even round number. I prayed and asked for the specific amount and the date that I needed it by, continued to thank the Lord for it, and looked forward to the provision, as it was so strong in my heart that it would be provided. The date I requested it by was on a Sunday, and the money had not arrived the day before that date, so I fully expected someone to bless us Sunday morning at church, but that didn't happen. Someone invited us to lunch, but again, no gift. We went to the Sunday evening service, and naturally, I fully expected to receive the gift there, but again, no gift. I vividly remember walking up the back stairs to our apartment talking to the Lord and questioning Him, since I didn't understand why the money didn't come. I was sad and disappointed, to say the least.

Well, when I got inside the apartment I looked and there was a message on the phone, the old type of phone on the wall—ha ha—which said to check my mailbox. So I went down the front stairs and reached inside the mailbox to find an envelope with the exact amount of money I prayed for! HALLELUJAH! I was ecstatic and praising and thanking the Lord!

◇ My landlord was aware that I was home praying and not working. My rent was not always paid on time, but I kept in touch with him, giving him as much information as I knew. He continued to trust that I would pay him; God gave me favor with him! When Holy Spirit put me back to work and I was able to move into an apartment on the third floor of the same building where I would be working, I let my landlord know immediately and added that I didn't have the last month's rent yet but would send it to him once I was paid. What he told me took me totally by surprise and very happy—he forgave me that last month's rent and I didn't have to pay it! WOW, another Hallelujah time!

Sensing a Transition

I attended some ministry classes at my church during that year and learned that a Bible school was being formed called Living Word Training Center. It would serve churches in the surrounding area and neighboring states, with classes available to train church leaders and individual believers to be better equipped for their service to others. I sensed to apply for the position of secretary, was hired, and started work on June 1, 1982.

It still amazes me that God had me home praying and trusting Him to meet our needs for exactly one year from June 1, 1981, and put me back to work on June 1, 1982! To me, being home exactly one year was also God vindicating my actions to those who didn't believe God called me to be home praying and trusting Him. Being so young in my Christian walk, that was important to me at that time.

I will be forever thankful for that year at home trusting in God as I learned early in my Christian life that God is faithful and especially when we obey His direction! He was truly my Jehovah Jireh, the Lord my Provider, during this time and continues to be Jehovah Jireh to me today.

Chapter 7

Living Word Training Center and Next Step

I was filled with excitement to be a part of a new ministry, knowing God opened this door for me, and I looked forward to this next chapter in my life and to seeing what all He had planned for me.

God had us move from Ephrata, to Mount Joy, into the same building where the training center was located. See more about this providential move in Chapter 8.

As you can imagine, there was an endless number of communications that needed to be done, and a myriad of details to process prior to the actual start of classes in the fall. Preparing the student catalog, which communicated purpose, vision, administration, information on teachers, curriculum information, course descriptions, general information and policies, and other information, was a big project.

I took all the information down for the student catalog from the President and Dean, Keith E. Yoder, Ed.D, in shorthand and typed it using a typewriter since we didn't have computers, which were only becoming popular in the 1980s. I was so thankful I had three years of shorthand and typing in high school and continued to use both over the next twenty years prior to starting work at Living Word Training Center (LWTC). Keith, as many people know, is an excellent instructor and taught many of the classes too.

During my time of serving at the training center, I was coordinator for the prayer team, and became the administrator and business manager, the position Dan Smucker held until he sensed the Lord directing him on to other things. Dan was the person who had the original vision for the training center, and God had put many things on his heart he wanted to accomplish.

As the business manager, working with numbers on this scale was new to me, and I discovered a love for it and took care of all the finances for the last couple of years LWTC was open. Everything was done by hand and a calculator and then typed back in those days. I was also the cleaning lady and, thankfully, had help at times. We did hire another receptionist/secretary, Karen Myer—Karen Myer Jackson now—when I moved into the new position, which was a big help! She did a great job and was a worshipper, played a couple of different instruments, and helped lead worship at the beginning of classes at times. Herbert Stoner was the assistant dean and was also an instructor and led worship at times. I loved when he led worship and played the piano; I would go lean against the piano and would feel like I became of part of the music. I have always loved listening to the piano.

Bob and Carolyn Thomas had a vision for a training center in Kennett Square for several years, which was fulfilled when a Branch Living Word Training Center was established there. Bob was the assistant dean and an instructor, and Carolyn was the administrative assistant and congregational relations coordinator for both locations. A part-time receptionist/secretary also served at the Branch location.

My first time ever out of the United States was to Haiti in 1984 for a much-needed vacation, rest, and refreshment due to all the hours worked since the start of the training center. We visited Christina Hawthorne, the first graduate of LWTC, who became a missionary in Haiti after graduating from the training center, and who also needed a time of rest and refreshment.

The following year, I went to Haiti a second time to help set up financial records for the start of The Haiti Discipling Center, which was the vision of Bob and Carolyn Thomas. I traveled with Bob and Carolyn on both trips to Haiti and will never forget how we had to run to catch a connecting flight on my first trip with them. Many good things happened in Haiti, and it was an eye-opening experience seeing how the people lived there!

I also enrolled as a student in the prophetic

ministry major and completed that study and graduated the last year the training center was in operation. We didn't know it at the start, but it was God's plan for the training center to only be in existence for five years. A lot was accomplished in the lives of many people and ministries during those five years, not only locally but in other parts of the world as well.

Opened Our Home to a Family in Need

Duane and Nancy Leatherman were missionaries in Belize, and Duane attended some classes at LWTC while they were home on furlough in 1982. They went back to Belize when the furlough was over. In the spring of 1984 while still serving in Belize, Duane was having some physical issues and was diagnosed with Guillain-Barre Syndrome, a rare condition in which a person's immune system attacks the peripheral nerves.

Duane ended up in the hospital, which is normal for people with Guillain-Barre Syndrome, but the hospital Duane was at in Belize didn't have the necessary equipment to treat Duane if his case proceeded to a certain point, so the mission board had him and Nancy and their son flown to a hospital in Florida. There was a medical accident while in the Florida hospital and Duane experienced cardiac and respiratory arrest, which caused a longtime comatose condition. When Keith and Dan heard about what happened to Duane, their immediate response was to fly to Florida to visit and pray for him. I was invited to go along to be a support to Nancy.

It was discussed about getting Duane transferred to a hospital in Lancaster, to be closer to the leadership of the sending mission board and others who knew the family. Nancy didn't have any relatives living in Lancaster County and wouldn't have a place to live when that transfer happened, so I offered to have her and her two-year-old son, Brian, come and live with us in our two-bedroom apartment on the third floor of the building where the training center was located. Nancy slept in the bed with me, and Brian slept on one of the couches. The other bedroom was my daughter's. Oh, Nancy was into her ninth month of pregnancy when she arrived in Pennsylvania at the beginning of June and had their daughter on June 24,

1984! There were forty-nine steps up and down to my apartment every time Nancy went somewhere, so we figured that helped her have a fairly easy delivery. I went through the delivery of her daughter with Nancy at the same hospital Duane was in, so, shortly after the delivery, I was able to go and tell him that he was now the father of a beautiful daughter named Beth.

Nancy was encouraged by the mission organization to seek legal advice due to the accident. A settlement included money to provide a home and the basic necessities of life for Nancy and the children. Duane ended up in the hospital for over fifteen years. Nancy was a very strong woman of faith and a devoted wife. For all those years he was in the hospital, Nancy visited Duane almost every day and would read the Word, worship, pray, tell him about the children and what was happening in all their lives, and other things. She was, and is, an amazing person!

There were people all over the world praying, asking God to heal Duane, but He didn't, and Duane went home to be with Jesus on November 8, 1999. We don't know or understand why God didn't answer the thousands of prayers that were prayed for Duane over all those years, but He didn't. God's faithfulness to Nancy and the children has never ceased!

Nancy and the children ended up living with us for a year and a half until a settlement was made with the hospital in Florida and she could purchase a home, furniture, and other necessities for her family. After eighteen months of living together, we were both looking forward to having our own places again. We have remained friends over all these years since that time.

The Thought of Putting a Knife into My Heart

For years whenever I would be handling a sharp, long-bladed knife, the thought would cross my mind about putting the knife into my heart! I didn't want to think that, had no idea why I thought it, but I couldn't control it or stop it from happening.

One time at the apartment in Ephrata, my daughter, who would have been around twelve or thirteen, and I were doing the dishes. She was drying a sharp, long-bladed knife, and I looked at her and said, "You'd like to put that in me, wouldn't you?" I could not believe I said those words to her! She ran into her room crying, and I went after her saying I'm sorry and don't know why I said that, and probably said a lot more, but don't recall my words. Oh, how I regretted those words! It bothered me deeply. I'm hoping she doesn't even recall them.

After the LWTC started, I heard about inner healing and how it can deal with things from the past and negative things affecting us. I purchased a book by John and Paul Sandford called *Transformation of the Inner Man,* released in 1982.[2] When reading a certain chapter in the book, the following thought crossed my mind: **my mother desired to abort me in the womb and that would have been putting a knife into me!** I prayed about it and knew I was to contact a friend, Ruth Ann Stauffer, about going through inner healing for this. A prayer time was scheduled, and there were a couple of other people there too.

During the prayer session, Ruth Ann said she sensed she was to sit in as proxy for my mother, who would have been dead for over thirty years at that time. When she started praying, I said I felt like I was to sit on her lap; she responded I was supposed to, so I did. She prayed and asked for forgiveness as proxy for my mom, and I forgave her. She continued in prayer and was singing and hugging me and speaking soft, tender words to me, and I cried like a baby! Crying was not something I did often, so this was so new to me. I had no memory of my mother ever holding and speaking tenderly to me. As previously shared, I only have three memories of her, and they were not pleasant ones. I sat on Ruth Ann's lap crying for a long, long time, and felt like a mother's love was being transferred to me and knew when I got back up off her lap that something was different inside of me and I was healed! Thank You, Father!

  The proof of that inner healing was that from that time on, whenever I handled a sharp, long-bladed knife, I never ever had thoughts of putting a knife into my heart again! One of the first things I did was share what happened with my daughter and explain that I couldn't help my thoughts or those words I spoke to her several years before, but I was now free, and it wasn't affecting me anymore. I'm sure I would have asked forgiveness again too. Hallelujah!

Life Changing and Saving Prophetic Ministry Class Assignment

A homework assignment was given to pray and seek the Lord regarding something to do with our family and then to prophesy about it. As I was praying, what came out of my mouth was this:

I was to give my daughter over to the Lord— that He was big enough to take care of her, so I gave her over to Him and His care!

This prophecy happened when my daughter and I were going through a very rough time for a long time. We were what some considered opposites in giftings, her mercy and me prophetic, so we butted heads a lot, so to speak. I didn't know how to be a good mom to her either, since it wasn't modeled to me growing up, which didn't help our relationship. I was so very strict and wouldn't let her do so many things she wanted to do, but I found out later in life she did some of them behind my back anyhow. I know the strictness was passed down from my mom's mother and possibly from farther back in our genealogy. I only remember my mom speaking to me once when she was correcting me for something, which, I'm guessing, was when I would have been around three or four years old!

After becoming a Christian, I had a great desire to go to Israel and walk where Jesus walked. In 1986, I was given a $2,000 gift through the Training Center to go to Israel and was excited, but then had the desire to take my daughter on a trip for her high school graduation gift. When I asked the board for permission to do it, they said yes! We went to Hawaii and had a wonderful time together, and a time of healing between us as well. I don't recall exactly when she moved out after graduation and our trip, but I do know I shared something my mom did that was passed down to me since I did the same thing. I asked my daughter to forgive me and then broke the generational curse over her.

Fast forward about ten years to 1996 when I was house sitting for friends until their home was sold (more on that later). Theresa was married now and recently had their daughter, Allyssa Rose Cox. They came to visit me and shared the following:

After the birth of my granddaughter, my daughter had a pap test that came back abnormal, and tests showed she had cervical cancer! WOW, what a shock to my ears!

My immediate response after they left was to get on my face on the floor in prayer, and I reverently reminded God of the words He spoke to hand her over to Him—that He was big enough to take care of her, so I expected Him to take care of this and heal her.

After surgery, the doctors advised they had gotten all the cancer, but then at her follow-up visit, they advised the cancer was right up to the end of what they removed from her, so they weren't sure if they had gotten it all. Another surgery was scheduled, and again, I went directly to prayer reminding God of His words, that she was in His hands and care, and, again, I knew He was big enough to take care of her and I fully expected Him to take care of her and heal her.

Thankfully, they didn't find any more cancer, so I always share that God either healed her or His Master surgical ability had the doctors cut the cancer off right at the very end of it! Either way, I will always praise and thank God for that prophecy and for saving her life!

Chapter 8

God's Predetermined Places for Me to Live and Work and His Providence Guiding Me to Them

I love this quote and can testify that it certainly has been true in my life!

"If you seek nothing but the will of God, He will always put you in the right place at the right time."[3] —Smith Wigglesworth

June 1982 to June 1988 in Mount Joy, PA

The location of LWTC was in Mount Joy, and I was living in Ephrata, so I asked the owner of the building I would be working in if any of the apartments on the third floor were available or would be available soon. He advised there weren't any available and wasn't aware that anyone was planning to move. Well, within days the landlord called me to say the people with the largest apartment, which had two bedrooms, were moving out and asked if I was interested in looking at it. Naturally, my answer was yes, and we moved into the apartment after it was vacated. Later, I learned that the people decided to move out when they found out a Bible school was being started because they didn't want to be that close to God! Wow, God surely opened that door for us!

As previously stated, the Training Center was only in operation for five years, and I ended up living at the Mount Joy location for another year, partially due to being responsible for closing things up at the Training Center and due to an apartment lease.

Seeking Guidance to Know Where My Next Job Was Going to Be

When it was definite that the Training Center was going to be closing, I knew God knew where I was going to work next, but I had no idea, so I asked

Him to advise me of what I was to do. One night in a dream, I saw myself talking to someone I knew at church who owned a business, asking him about work. I called him the next day and told him about the dream, and he advised me to call his brother, who was a co-owner of the business. I called the brother, and he hired me on a part-time basis, doing industrial cleaning at various companies, and a lot of work was done for a very large floor manufacturing company. This was so out of the norm for me, since I had only ever worked in an office, but I learned a lot and enjoyed the work even if I didn't look like, or feel like, a woman when I left work due to the safety clothing, helmet, and so forth that were necessary for the work and wearing boots instead of nice shoes with heels. Plus, I sweated a lot while using a power grinder to clean black baked-on material off the walls and other equipment inside big industrial ovens that the linoleum went through to have the coatings on them dried. I also sweated a lot being up in the air cleaning dirt off the top of ductwork in print rooms for a large printing company, and a multitude of other jobs at other companies, and just plain got dirty and all disheveled! I learned a lot about power tools and mechanical stuff in this position, and I'm very thankful for this knowledge; I love power tools now!

I ended up working my way up to be in charge of the industrial cleaning part of the company. After a couple of years, I knew I was training one of the people I hired to be able to take over my position, but not knowing what my future would be. Then, when a woman in the office left, I started working in the office on a temporary basis until someone else was found to take her place, however, that temporary position ended up lasting twenty-five years, and a total of twenty-eight years with the company until a freak accident happened at my home in 2015—more on the accident later.

June 1988 to June 1996 in Lancaster, PA

From Mount Joy, I moved to an apartment complex in Lancaster, which was close to the main highways with easy access to where I was working.

Direction to Sell Everything and Give to the Poor

Early in 1996, Holy Spirit started ministering to me to sell my personal belongings and give the money to the poor! WOW, I knew this was in the Word but never heard of anyone doing it except in the Word. I had a very hard time accepting this direction because I purchased a lot of very nice furniture when I moved into the apartment, and I loved my furniture. Plus, I questioned if this really was Holy Spirit speaking to me since it wasn't a normal thing people were doing. I understood people not being able to encourage me to do it. I struggled and prayed about it a lot, but Holy Spirit just kept encouraging me to walk in faith and do it. It took a while, but when I finally said yes to Holy Spirit that I would do what He asked me to do, I can't explain the freedom and joy and peace that I experienced! It was beyond words!

I had so much joy in selling and giving to others in need. Some things were given directly to people in need, and a couple of things were donated to different ministries with the understanding that they would, in turn, bless someone else who they knew needed help. All my beautiful living room and dining room furniture went very quickly, and it didn't bother me a bit! After a couple of weeks when most of my furniture was gone, I was released inside from the directive to sell and give. What was left was my waterbed, a lamp from my bedroom, my office desk and equipment, and some odds and ends from the kitchen. The only place I could sit down was on a chair in my office.

June 1996 to Summer 1997 in Lancaster, PA

I had no idea what God had planned and where I was going to live, but then I received a phone call from a friend who advised me they were moving to western Pennsylvania and wanted to know if I would housesit their condominium until it sold and make sure it was all cleaned up for when home showings were scheduled. And then she shared,

I would not have to pay any rent!

Wow! I only would be responsible to pay the utilities! My answer, of course, was a big yes! And then she shared that they were leaving almost all the furniture in the home so it showed better when people came to look at it!

Another Wow! It all made sense now why God had me sell my furniture! There was an empty room available in the basement where I set up my office desks, an old metal one and a large wooden top piece with side panels, and equipment so I could continue my studies there. Since I didn't have to pay rent, it worked out that I could reduce my hours at the office where I was working and could do most of my reduced responsibilities from home, which was great!

My waterbed, which came apart into four large drawer sections that were placed on top of each other, the rest of the bed, and boxes with other odds and ends could be stored in that room as well. In the future, I stacked the waterbed bottom drawers on top of each other in two sections, had an Amish neighbor make a top and sides for it, and turned it into a 7-1/2' long bureau for my bedroom. It has an amazing amount of storage in it.

It took about a year for a contract to be signed and the sale of the home.

So again, the question was, "Where am I going to live now, Lord?"

Summer of 1997 to End of 1999 in Gordonville, PA

It didn't take long before someone approached me and asked if I was interested in living in their basement apartment. I knew immediately that my answer was to be yes. So, again, my Father had a place all prepared for me to move to. Now I had to buy some furniture, and I ended up going back to my position at the office full-time without losing any of my benefits from cutting my hours back while house-sitting, so I was going to have money to buy furnishings. One of the first things I bought was a pink La-Z-Boy Glider Recliner that had a 360-degree full swivel. Twenty-five years later, this is still my favorite chair and is the one I sit in all the time and do most of my reading and praying on it. I also purchased a small leaf table for the kitchen and three chairs, which several years later turned into a table to hold my sewing machine in my ER, my Everything Room, so named since it served a multitude of purposes.

Next was the purchase of a couch, and boy did my taste in the style of furniture change from what I had previously. It went from a low-back, curved couch to a straight couch with a high back. I love flowers so, yep, my couch is custom covered with bright, vibrant colors of various types of flowers and greenery on it; I absolutely love it. I also love being able to sit and have my whole back and head against the couch and know it is healthier since it gives support for both lower and upper back and I don't slouch down. Twenty-five years later, I'm still using it and loving it.

The apartment was nice-sized, with several rooms and storage areas, and it had a separate outside entrance. The surrounding area in front of the home was beautiful farmland!

After a couple of years, the owner of the home was building an addition on to the other side of the home so his mother could come live there. She and her husband either built the home or had it built, but a number of years after her husband died, she sold it to one of her sons. She then enjoyed living in her beautiful double-wide modular home, but after several years when her son offered to build an addition on to the home so she could return there, she agreed to it.

Then I was advised that the township would not allow three kitchens in the home, so I would have to move and be out by January 1, 2000, also known as Y2K!

**So again, the question was,
"Where am I going to live now, Lord?"**

The home I was living in was right behind the home of the owners of a restaurant. I would say hi to the wife while out walking, and we would chat occasionally. One day I told her I was going to have to move and asked her to keep me in mind if she knew of any places available or heard of any from people who frequented their restaurant. She was a very outgoing person and loved talking to people. It wasn't long before she heard of two places, and she took me to see them, but we both knew they were not the right places for me, which was interesting since she didn't really know me well. So, back to seeking Holy Spirit's guidance and waiting!

It was getting close to the end of December 1999, and I still didn't know where I was going. My heart's cry was, "Father, I know You are never late, but I really need to know where I'm going since I need to be out of the apartment I was living in by the end of December." Yes, I was a little anxious, but I knew in my heart God had it all under control. Then, within a couple of days, I received a phone call from the woman who had taken me to see the places that I mentioned previously, and she advised me they were going to build a new home about a mile away and would I be interested in living in it! Of course, I said yes, not knowing anything about the house!

The home was going to take several months to build, so now I needed to find a place to live until it was built.

So again, the question was, "Where am I going to live now, Lord?"

January 2000 to August 25, 2000 in Manheim, PA

I told good friends what was happening, and they ended up sharing they had a room that I could live in until the new home was built and that I could have my cat, Abraham, there too.

I rented a storage unit to put almost all my furniture in since there was a bed in the room I'd be spending most of my time in while living in my friends' home. I am very thankful for my brother and the truck he used in his produce business along with other family and neighbors who helped pack my belongings into his truck to take my possessions to the storage unit.

A lot of time was spent in my room when not at work since I didn't want to interrupt my friends' normal routine, but we did have great times together too. They shared meals with me as well. When they made popcorn in the evening, the aroma would call me to go downstairs, and they always shared some with me.

In the beginning, as the new home was being built, I made occasional visits to see how the progress was going, which was not going as quickly as expected. I started making bi-weekly and then weekly visits later and took pictures of different stages of the build. I wanted to be a part of it in some way and asked the owners what I could do to help and ended up filling nail holes with wood filler in preparation for painting.

After eight months, the home was finally completed and ready for me to move into it. Hallelujah!

August 25, 2000, to April 1, 2019 in Gordonville, PA

August 25, 2000, was my fifty-sixth birthday, so what an amazing birthday present from the Lord to move into a brand-new home! Thank You, Father!

The 2800 square foot Cape Cod home was the fifth home built in a new development in Intercourse, Pennsylvania, and located in such a beautiful setting with an amazing view of farmland out back. I have amazing photos of sunrises that I love. Abraham, my cat, had a lot of windows and sunlight to enjoy again after being in one room for eight months! I got

Abraham and his sister, Sarah, when they were little kittens, and they both fit into one hand. Naturally, they had to have faith names! Sarah died several years before, so it was just me and Abraham. The garage was a two vehicle one but was extra wide and extra deep; it probably would have easily fit three vehicles in it, and again, it was extra deep as well. I loved all that space.

I had prayed and thanked God for several years to provide a big, beautiful home that I could call my own and decorate the way I wanted to, and I knew this home was the answer to those prayers. I also knew in my heart that God answered those prayers due to my obedience in selling and giving to the poor several years prior! I just marveled and was in awe of His provision and continue to be to this day! Oh, the rent I paid was unbelievably low; they could have easily charged three times what they were charging me for the size of the home and being a brand-new home. Again, I believe that was a part of God's reward for the obedience to sell and give to the poor. Mark 10:30, states, **"Who will not receive a hundred**

times as much now in this time—houses and brothers and sisters and mothers and children and lands, with persecutions—and in the age to come, eternal life."

Again, I enjoyed shopping for furniture since there was a dining room and I didn't have any dining room furniture, plus purchased patio and porch furniture and a lot of other miscellaneous things, including a good Hoover self-propelled upright vacuum that I'm still using over twenty-two years later. I like purchasing quality things that last for years.

I took care of the home like it was my own and had learned to love pressure washing things a couple of years before, so purchasing a pressure washer was a must. Memorial Day week ended up being an annual vacation week for me from work and I would pressure wash the exterior of the home, patio and porch furniture, rugs, and a plethora of other things. The vegetable garden and flower planting would also be done during that week. I loved having a lot of beautiful flower plants on the porch, not only for me to enjoy but for the neighbors too. Neighbors often commented on how beautiful it was and that they enjoyed seeing it. I had a lot of flower plants on the patio in the back of the home as well and planted beautiful flowers in the flower beds and enjoyed taking pictures of them. The owners had beautiful landscape planted when the home was built, and over the years I added several different types of bushes.

I developed a love for rocks, which were plentiful since there was a lot of blasting going on due to hitting rock underground with other new homes being built in the development. I collected a lot of them, pressure washed them, and incorporated their beauty into the flower beds and on the porch and patio. There was one big, boulder-like rock that I loved, but I couldn't carry it. I envisioned it on the front porch near the front door. A guy on a skid loader passed by one day, and I asked him if he would do me a favor and get a huge rock and drop it on the street in front of my home, and he did! I was so happy, but now how do I move it approximately twenty feet to get it across the grass and up an incline to get it on the porch? I rolled it across the grass and even rolled it up the step to get it on the porch—success!

On occasion, I would invite people to come for a meal, but due to the long hours I was working for many years while living there, I was the main person who got to enjoy it. When my granddaughter was young, she would come and spend some weekends with me; I thoroughly enjoyed those times. We watched children's Christian VCR tapes together and other children's tapes on occasion as well. After watching one of the Christian tapes and me explaining to her about Jesus, I asked her if she wanted to accept Him, and she said yes! I told her that my anniversary of accepting Jesus was the next day on April 1 and asked if she wanted to wait until then, but she said, "No, I want to do it now." So we prayed, and she accepted Jesus as her Savior on March 31, 2001! What a blessing to be a part of that!

Being a Blessing to My Landlords

My landlord advised me in the spring of 2002 that he and his wife were planning to go to Romania for a year to serve as missionaries with their daughter, who was already serving there. I sensed to volunteer to take care of their finances while they were gone. They were thankful for my offer and agreed to have me do it. Power of attorney at the bank was signed over to me, and all their mail transferred to my address. This was going to be a new experience for me, and I looked forward to serving them in this way.

They were grateful that all went well while they were in Romania, and when they got home, they told me I didn't have to pay the next month's rent. They were blessing me back for volunteering to help them. Wow, I didn't expect that; I was thankful for the blessing.

A Life-Changing Surrender

During the week of October 8, 2017, I heard when spending time with the Lord,

"Make room in your heart for more of Me."

On October 28, 2017, in the early a.m. while reading Tony Evans' book, *The Power of God's Names*[4], after finishing the chapter on Adonai, which means Lord and Master and the God Who rules, I prayed a prayer of surrender, which was not the first one I ever prayed. What I heard inside immediately was:

"**No TV for a week.**"

My thoughts were, **oh, no, Hallmark's Christmas movies were going to start that evening, and I always watch them.** The only thing was while watching them and, especially after they ended, I cried and cried because I was alone and wasn't experiencing the happiness they were in the movies. Normally I wasn't unhappy, nor did I have the feeling of being alone; I only had those thoughts and feelings while watching those movies.

I went to bed in the wee hours of the morning on the twenty-eighth and heard the same thing as I was getting up, so yes, it was from my Adonai, and I surrendered and was obedient! I had been spending hours weekly watching the news, HGTV shows, and Hallmark movies, so this was going to be a big change!

I was reminded of what the Lord said earlier in the month to make room in my heart for more of Him, and no TV would enable that to happen.

The whole first day of no TV was spent praying, listening for Holy Spirit, listening to sermons, and reading. It was a wonderful day, and I didn't miss TV at all!

One week led to another and another of no TV, and I never missed it and still don't miss it and am sure I never will. My granddaughter ended up with the big screen TV that had been purchased within the last year.

No TV opened so much more time to study to know God more deeply and intimately, and especially through the meanings of His names. I have read and reread and taken notes from Tony Evans' book, *The Power of God's Names,* and am so thankful for this book. I also love his book, The Power of Jesus' Names, too.[4]

The knowledge of God is so important! Look at some of the amazing benefits from knowing Him from 2 Peter 1:2-3:

May grace (God's favor) and peace (which is perfect well-being, all necessary good, all spir-

itual prosperity, and freedom from fears and agitating passions and moral conflicts) be multiplied to you in [the full, personal, [precise, and correct] knowledge of God and of Jesus our Lord.

For His divine power has bestowed upon us all things that [are requisite and suited] to life and godliness, through the full, personal] knowledge of Him Who called us by and to His own glory and excellence (virtue).

There are so many other Scriptures that talk about knowing God too. I encourage us all to search them out and grow in the knowledge of God and know that He has a perfect plan for our lives that He will bring about as we trust and rely on Him and Holy Spirit to guide our thoughts and steps into His will for our lives.

Change Was on the Horizon

On July 17, 2018, my landlord of eighteen years called and advised me that his grandson and wife wanted to look at the home I was living in, and they were coming that very night. My first response was, **oh no**, but my second response was one of excitement and wondering what God was up to now.

It still amazes me that I even pressure washed the north side of the house and the very dirty exterior steps to the basement on Sunday, July 15, since I would never do that kind of stuff on a Sunday. Then on Monday, July 16, I finished pressure washing the walkway, so the whole exterior looked great. Then I received the call on the 17th that they were coming to look at the home that evening. Wow, God was preparing things ahead of time for when they came to look at it!

There was no way they wouldn't like the home, as it was a beautiful and spacious 2800+ square foot home, a beautiful farmland view in the back, and in a lovely neighborhood with good neighbors.

Well, then thoughts started entering my mind about how much I loved it there, and I started trying to figure out a way I could earn additional income and pay more rent and continue to live there. Due to the accident I was involved in back in 2015, (more on the accident later) and unable to walk for close to three months, I lost my job of twenty-eight years, which turned out to be a good thing, and was living almost entirely on Social Security payments. I asked my landlord if I could earn more money in some way and pay more rent would I be able to continue living there. He told me his relatives still hadn't advised him if they wanted to live there or not.

One day while mowing the grass, I sensed the grace of God to live there was leaving. Holy Spirit let me know inside that I would be moving, so freedom once again ruled my heart and mind, and I started looking with anticipation and excitement to see what the Lord had planned for the next part of my journey. I felt kind of like a nomad moving from one place to another and never knowing how long I would be at one place, but I wouldn't trade my life for one living in a castle as my faith and trust continues to grow living the life God prepared for me!

Soon after Holy Spirit let me know I would be moving, I went to my landlord's home to lend him a medical device to use since he was dealing with a medical issue. His grandson and wife came up from the basement where they had been living for a couple of years to learn about the medical device too. As we were all sitting around the table talking, I told them all that I knew inside that I would be moving out of the house. The grandson commented that they didn't know if they were going to move in yet, but if they would, they wouldn't want to move in until April 1, 2019; wow, another special April 1 in the making for me! I didn't hear any definite answer for weeks if they wanted to move into the home or not, so I called my landlord. He advised me that yes, they wanted to move into the home. They wanted to rent it, not purchase it.

So again, the question was, "Where am I going to live now, Lord?"

Having an eight-month advance notice that I would be moving out of the home didn't put pressure on me to prepare for the move, so when I started looking for a place to move to in early 2019, I discovered it wasn't going to be easy because most places were through rental agencies, which I don't recall ever having used in my life. To qualify to rent through a rental agency, you had to be able to show monthly income three times the amount of the rental charge and have proof of that income for the three previous months! The only income I had was social security payments, which meant that I would only be eligible to rent a place for around $650 a month, and there wasn't much available in that rental range. I looked for places online and did physically visit several places but couldn't believe what was available in my price range! Plus, there would also be additional charges for water and sewer, trash disposal, as well as needing to mow and/or be responsible for snow removal. What a reality check after living in a big, beautiful home for over eighteen years with a very low monthly rent amount, which was a total blessing from God as previously mentioned! I had also checked with friends to see if they knew of anyone who had something available, but no positive responses were received.

Waiting on Holy Spirit's Guidance

I kept asking Holy Spirit to guide me to the place He had for me, but I wasn't getting any direction. When I knew I would be moving, I asked my

Father to please let me know ahead of time where I would be going and not to have to wait until it was time to move and then kept thanking Him for doing it, but He didn't do it! He was probably sitting on His throne laughing at my request and thinking, **but that wouldn't require walking in faith and trusting Me!**

In the beginning of March 2019, I was getting a little concerned since I still didn't know where I was moving to, so I called my landlord and told him I still didn't have a place. During our conversation, he mentioned something about how God's timing is not always our timing. I took those words to mean that it would be all right if I wasn't out by April 1 and was happy about that since there was an annual development yard sale toward the end of April and I wanted to be able to participate in that and get a lot of things ready to sell.

On March 20 or 21, 2019, there was a knock on my front door; my landlord's son was outside, strongly encouraging me to be out of the house by April 1. He mentioned legal proceedings were possible if I wasn't out! When the conversation was over, I immediately sought the Lord and asked for help and guidance, but heaven was silent! On March 22, 2019, there was a knock on my patio door, and it was my landlord. We had a short conversation and the potential for legal proceedings was mentioned again. He then handed me an envelope with a paragraph typed on a sheet of paper, again stressing that I needed to be out. I kept apologizing and advising that the Lord hadn't provided anything yet.

Again, I was back to asking the Lord what I'm supposed to do, and I sensed I needed to call my daughter and send her a copy of what my landlord wrote. After reading it, she said, "We must get you out of there." She advised me they didn't have room, since someone was living with them, but they would work something out and I could stay with them if nothing else was available, and then she asked if there was someone I could move in with for a while. I mentioned my friend, Ann Dienner, had advised me a while back that they had several bedrooms that weren't being used, and she would talk to her husband, Amos, about me living there for a while until I found a place to live, but I never heard anything back about it and I didn't bring it up again. My daughter said I needed to ask her, so I called and told her what was happening. She said she'd talk to Amos and get back to me within twenty-four hours. In less than twenty-four hours, I received a call from Ann advising me that Amos said yes. She told me that he had said,

I wouldn't have to pay any rent!

Wow, thank You, Father! Again, He had everything worked out in advance! I immediately called my daughter and then my landlord and told him I had found a place to live for a while and that I'd be out by April 1. Naturally, he was curious and asked where I was going, and I told him I was moving in with friends. He was glad to hear it was all working out.

So Much to Accomplish in a Week!

Thinking I was going to be in the house longer and be able to participate in the yard sale, I still had a lot of stuff to pack, so the race was on to be out of the house in a week! So many things needed done, including but limited to:

◇ Finding a rental storage unit that could hold about 95 percent or more of my personal belongings, which ended up being a 12' wide x 12' high x 30' deep unit.

◇ Renting a much smaller storage unit to store things for a short time I knew I'd be selling.

◇ Comparing pricing and finding a truck to facilitate the move to the storage units and several items to my friend's home where I'd be living. I'm so thankful that my large upright freezer with a lot of food in could go in their basement too!

◇ Packing, packing, and more packing; and had to make several trips to stores to purchase more totes.

◇ My daughter, Theresa Fackler, recruited people to come and help pack and load and unload the truck during the actual move.

◇ My granddaughter, Allyssa Cox, recruited a couple of friends, and they packed up a lot of my office and things from in my bedroom and helped load and unload the truck too.

⋄ My stepdaughter, Dani, and her husband, Cameron Rider, were a huge help packing and at other times too. After I gave her permission, Dani really enjoyed throwing away a lot of my stuff that hadn't been used in a long time.

⋄ I gave away a lot of things to people who helped with the move, which was a blessing to them and to me since I love giving.

The final move took place on Sunday, March 31, 2019, which was in no way a normal thing for me to be doing on a Sunday, but sometimes you just must do what you must do! It ended up being a very windy and cold day, but thankfully it wasn't raining or snowing. I'm so very thankful for my son-in-law, Chuck Fackler, and a friend of Theresa and Chuck's named Greg Ritter for their strategic planning and excellent stacking skills at the big storage unit! Boxes and totes were stacked almost up to the top of the 12' high unit for at least a quarter or more of the depth of the unit at the back. Chuck and Greg just flowed so well together, not only at the back of the unit but placing items in the whole unit; it looked like they had been doing this together for a long time, but this was their first time! Others were a great help too in unloading things from the truck and putting them into the unit to be placed by Chuck and Greg.

There is no way that move could have been facilitated in such a short amount of time without my daughter and son-in-law; Greg; my granddaughter; my stepdaughter and her husband; and my friend, Ann, whose home I was moving into temporarily; and all the other people who helped in any way! I continue to be grateful for everyone's help, and especially to my Heavenly Father, Who orchestrated everything!

My landlord had previously given approval for me to be there on April 1, so on March 31, after everything was unloaded, and everyone left the storage unit, I went back to the house and slept on the floor of what was my bedroom so I could tidy things up a bit on April 1. My bedroom furniture had not been moved for over eighteen years, so needless to say there were rolls of dust along the walls after everything was out of the room, and I just couldn't leave that there, even though the owners said it was all right since they were going to be doing some sanding and painting. I didn't remove all the buildup but did get a good amount of it. The grandson moving into the home said it was okay if I left some things there, and if they didn't want them, they would take care of them for me, so there were some things in the garage I wanted to go through yet too.

My landlord had asked if I minded if they were at the house on April 1 while I was there so they could start filling nail holes in the walls and sanding in preparation for painting and work on some other things, and naturally, I said, no, I didn't mind. Our relationship was already restored and there were no hard feelings between us at all, which was great! They ended up leaving before I did on April 1.

When I finally left in the early evening of April 1, my Honda CRV was packed to the top with things I wanted to take with me from the garage. I sent a couple of photos to my daughter and son-in-law, boasting about my awesome packing skills, and they were shocked that I loaded it up with more stuff!

Living in that home was a great blessing from the Lord and I will be forever grateful for that experience!

Hindsight

Thinking back on all that happened, I am so glad that God didn't answer my repeated prayers asking Him to let me know where I was moving before the time I had to move. If He would have done that, I would not have, once again, had to walk by faith and get to experience His providential care for me and see His plan unfold. He is Sovereign and knew exactly where I would end up. Even though He was silent regarding my prayers, He was still working in the silence to get me where I needed to be and was working out the steps to get me there. As the Word says in **Proverbs 16:9, "A man's mind plans his way, but the Lord directs his steps and makes them sure."**

God wants us to know Him through His names

and His character, which He reveals in the Word, and He also wants us to know Him through our own individual experiences with Him here on this earth as we walk by faith trusting and relying on Him as our Source for all things! Romans 15:13, states, **"May the God of your hope so fill you with all joy and peace in believing [through the experience of your faith] that by the power of the Holy Spirit you may abound and be overflowing (bubbling over) with hope."**

April 1, 2019, to May 5, 2019, in Ronks, PA

All I can say is *wow* regarding the next several days and seeing God's amazing providential care being prepared ahead of time for me, and Holy Spirit guiding my steps to be exactly where I was meant to be!

This was another amazing April 1 experience with the Lord, and it was also my fortieth anniversary of accepting Jesus as my Savior too!

The chair I always sat in, a light, a small shelf unit and several other things were previously moved to the bedroom in my friend's home where I'd be staying for an undetermined amount of time. The evening of April 1, Ann and I were making the bed that I was going to sleep in and while spreading out a sheet I had a knowing inside that I had done this exact same thing before, even though I had not done it in the natural. Holy Spirit was letting me know I was right where I was supposed to be!

The very next day, Amos called and advised me that he was reminded of a friend who had rental properties. He called his friend and inquired if he had anything available, and the answer was yes. There was an apartment that would be available on April 15 and rent for $700 a month, which included water and sewer and trash removal and tenants were not responsible for cutting grass or snow removal! If I was interested, I should call his office and set up a time to see it with his rental manager. Wow, of course I was interested and did see the apartment a couple of days later. When I walked inside the apartment, I had a knowing inside that this was my next home. I sensed the living room area would be big enough that I could split it up and make half my living area and half my office area that my big U-shaped desk could fit in. I did go back and measure regarding the desk to make sure it would fit, and indeed, it would. There were two bedrooms, and a nice size kitchen for a small apartment where my large upright freezer would fit as well. One of the bedrooms would turn into what I called an ER, an everything room, which is an amazing space to have.

I contacted the owner and told him I'd like to rent the apartment. He then advised me that his wife had someone else who wanted to rent it, but if I would pay for half a month's rent for April I could have it, and I said, yes, I would pay it. Another amazing thing about this is that I didn't have to prove I had a certain amount of income to be able to rent this place either! Wow, thank You, Father, that once again, You had this all planned out ahead of time for me!

I also advised the landlord of the home I just moved out of how God provided, and he and his wife were happy for me. They experienced God's amazing provision for similar things in their life too.

May 5, 2019, to Present in Leola, PA

Oh my, we just finished moving all that stuff into storage and now we were going to be moving certain things out of storage and into the apartment. I am so thankful for my family and friends to facilitate moving stuff again in such a short amount of time! My king-size mattress and box springs wouldn't fit in the apartment bedroom, so I had to order a queen-size. I also had to wait to move when Chuck was off work, so that gave time to do cleaning at the apartment prior to moving in. My friend, Ann, helped on several occasions with cleaning—I'm so thankful for her help!

The move into the apartment was made easier due to Chuck's planning and strategy when moving things out of the big house and into the big storage unit. He arranged to keep the things I would need immediately for a new place at the front of the big storage unit for easy access, which worked great!

Then my next project after getting what I needed out of the storage unit was to go through everything that was left in the big storage unit and decide what was going to be transferred into a smaller climate-controlled unit I rented that was 10' wide x 10' high x 18' deep, and what I was going to sell, which was mainly at yard sales. Years ago, I had all my totes numbered and listed what was in them on 3" x 5" cards. It was so easy to find things because all I had to do was look through the cards for what I needed and then locate the tote with the number that was on the card. The totes started out being stacked pretty much in order. They didn't always end up back where they were taken from, but it was still easy just to look for a number rather than going through all the totes looking for something! But over the years, things were taken out of totes and the system was no longer being followed. So I had to go through everything and sort stuff. I was thankful I purchased a Little Giant ladder years ago for use at the house since I used that to maneuver totes and boxes down to the floor level so that I could go through them. Only once did I have to have help getting a couple of very large, heavy boxes down to floor level and was thankful for my stepdaughter's husband being available to come and help!

Apartment Living Again

It was an adjustment to go from living in a large, over 2800 square foot home to an apartment that was under 850 square feet, but I am just as happy and content here as I was at the big house. I enjoyed mowing the lawn and shoveling and snow blowing at the big house, but don't have to do any of that where I'm living now, and I've learned to appreciate that. I do have a back entrance, which I use as my main entrance, with a little deck and some grass surrounding the deck. I have been able to do a little gardening and am very thankful for that space. I love having lettuce, tomatoes, onions, herbs, and other things right outside my door to pick fresh and know there haven't been any chemicals sprayed on them! I even saved seeds from my plants one year and then started plants from those seeds the following year, which was a new experience for me, and I loved it. I still have seeds left for future use too.

Since my upright freezer fits in the kitchen, I've been able to make stewed tomatoes using tomatoes, peppers, and onions from my garden and freeze that, along with making fresh applesauce and other things and freezing them. There is a little table in my kitchen, but my sewing machine and other sewing supplies are on it, so I don't eat in the kitchen. I enjoy eating outside on the deck when possible; otherwise, I'm eating on my favorite chair in the living area or at my desk—it works for me.

There are eight small apartments in the building I'm living in now, which was an adjustment for me to be around more people, but I have gotten used to it. I also love having days totally to myself sometimes and not seeing or talking to anyone. Most apartments are rented by individuals who pretty much keep to themselves like me. I've had the opportunity to talk about the Lord with most of them.

I love living in this apartment and, as previously stated, I'm just as happy and content here as I was in the big house. However, I know change is coming sometime in the future.

Chapter 9

Divine Disruption on June 9, 2015

I was still working a fulltime-job when I was seventy and would often end up mowing in the evening after getting home from work.

On Tuesday, June 9, 2015, I came home from work and was mowing my grass. Prior to starting work on the backyard, I always stopped and got a drink of water from the fridge in the garage. Well, on this Tuesday, my life as I knew it drastically changed!

As I was stepping into the garage, my right ankle was hit by a little remote car, and I ended up falling forward onto the concrete garage floor on both knees and then fell backward and hit my head on the concrete floor. Things were a blur for a brief period, but I must have started screaming because my neighbor heard me and came over to see what happened. She saw the remote car in my garage and discovered her youngest son, who was six at the time, was trying to get a different car to work and was using the wrong remote. So the other car would have come down their driveway, crossed over a small patch of grass, and came up my driveway and hit me right as I was stepping into the garage. I'm guessing the car traveled forty-five feet or so from their place to my ankle! I did hear a loud noise, but then instantly I was on the garage floor.

My neighbor tried to help me stand, but there was too much pain in both legs. My thoughts were that something must have been sprained. I asked my neighbor to get a couple of frozen packs of veggies from the freezer in the garage so I could put them on my legs where they hurt. I held the frozen packages on my legs for a time and then tried to stand but could not due to the pain. I tried this several times with no success.

My neighbor suggested going to an urgent care, or if there was someone I could call, so I called my daughter and told her what happened. I'll never forget my daughter's words: "Mom, you're in a lot of pain and you can't walk, so what do you think you should do?" Yes, I knew I had to get it checked out. My neighbor agreed to take me to an urgent care near my daughter's home. My daughter and son-in-law met us there, and he proceeded to lift me out of my neighbor's vehicle and carry me inside. I was shocked he was able to do that because he's a skinny guy, but apparently all muscle!

The urgent care visit was not a pleasant experience! X-rays were taken, and the doctor said he looked at them and didn't think there were any breaks, but a person more qualified to look at x-rays was going to check them out. Then the doctor came in and said it looked like there was a small fracture in one of the legs. He wanted to send me home with crutches and advised me to see an orthopedic doctor. Well, there was no way I could use the crutches due to the pain in both legs, so off to the hospital emergency room we went where we waited for I don't know how many hours until it was my turn to be seen.

More x-rays were taken at the hospital that revealed both my tibia bones were fractured! I was admitted, but the surgeon wanted to wait a couple of days due to swelling in my legs before deciding what direction to take. Surgery was completed on both legs at the same time, and plates and screws were put in both legs! I had never had a broken bone in my life before, and now at age seventy, I had two of them! I was in the hospital for a week, a skilled nursing facility for seven weeks, and home most of the month of August with a wheelchair and walker to get around. I couldn't even try to walk for almost three months! After I was released to start walking, a couple of months of physical therapy followed.

In an instant, I became totally dependent on other people, which was difficult for me since I was very independent due to living alone for so many years and would do everything myself or find a way to accomplish whatever needed to be done. I was so thankful to be in a room by myself in the skilled nursing facility since I was used to being alone; always ate my meals in my room too. Thankfully, my daughter lived close to me and brought me necessities from home, and she or my granddaughter would take care of laundering my clothes. It was great to have my computer too, but I spent a lot of time alone, wondering why this happened, when would this be over, what was going to happen in my future. I thought of Psalm 23, where it says, **"He makes me lie down..."**; granted, it wasn't in fresh green pastures, but I did end up with an air bed due to my boney butt—He definitely made me lie down! I know a lot of people may not agree with me, and that's all right, but I know that little remote car was divinely guided to hit me, which resulted in some needed adjustments in my life happening. I knew God was in control and had a plan for my future, even though I didn't know or understand it back then!

Transition Time

For years, I took vacation every Memorial Day

week to pressure wash the house and a multitude of other things (I love pressure washing), planting my vegetable garden, planting flowers, and catching up on other tasks that needed to be done. In 2015, that week just happened to be the week before the accident, and I recall standing in front of the kitchen window looking out over the field and beautiful view behind my home and I said, "I can't wait until I can be home all the time." Little did I know, the following week something would happen that would enable that desire to be fulfilled, but certainly not in a way I expected!

I worked for the same company for twenty-eight years, but due to the accident and not being able to work for months, I lost my job, which ended up being a good thing!

I am so thankful that the accident happened! I loved most everything about my job and was devoted to it, and it was normally always on my mind even when I wasn't in the office. But my time with the Lord wasn't what it should have been since so much time was spent at my job or thinking about it.

The greatest thing that resulted from the accident was that I returned to my first love and now have hours with the Lord daily in the Word, in prayer, and memorizing Scriptures again, and I love it! My calling is prayer and I'm back to walking in that calling! And I wrote a book, which was totally unexpected.

Like Romans 8:28, says**, "We are assured and know that [God being a partner in their labor] all things work together and are [fitting into a plan] for good to and for those who love God and are called according to [His] design and purpose."** Amen to that! I am home again, literally and figuratively!

The Insurance Settlement

Since the accident was caused by my neighbor's son, their homeowners liability insurance was liable for the bills incurred because of the accident and for the pain and suffering that I went through. People kept giving me counsel to contact an attorney, which I didn't want to do because I had a good relationship with my neighbors and didn't want to ruin that. However, I ended up telling my neighbor this is what I was advised to do and was the route I was taking; he totally understood. My attorney advised me that I would have to sue them to get their insurance company to pay, which again, I didn't want to do, but had to do it.

I had prayed several times for God to speed up the settlement, but the dates I requested came and went without the settlement being completed. Then on March 2, 2016, about nine months after the accident, I was reading in Mark again, and when I got to chapter 11:23–24, I stopped and told the mountain to move that was blocking the settlement. Shortly after that, a call from my attorney's office came, advising me that my neighbor's insurance was paying the full policy limit and that everything should be over in two weeks or less! It didn't happen in two weeks, and I'm glad it didn't because God gave me another amazing April 1 experience!

On March 31, 2016, at 10:30 p.m., I opened a letter from my neighbor's insurance company, and inside were copies of the settlement checks sent to my attorney's office. On April 1, 2016, my attorney's office received the checks, and I went and signed the bigger one that was for me, since it was made out to both my attorney's office and me. They then mailed me a check from their office, and I received it the following week. Another amazing April 1 for me when the checks arrived!

The second check was made out directly to Medicare to reimburse them for the amount settled upon. My hospital bill for the week was over $100,000, which Medicare paid. Originally, Medicare was going to require a payback of over $34,000 from my settlement check, but my attorney's assistant got them to accept a little over $22,000, which was awesome! My attorney's fees were based on an hourly rate rather than a contingency fee, which was a savings to me too.

I was living in the big, beautiful home that God provided during this time and did not have any income coming in since, as previously stated, I couldn't work and lost my job, and was so grateful for the amazing favor God gave me with my landlord in that I didn't have to pay rent for ten months until the settlement check came. When the settlement came, I immediately wrote him a check for twelve months of rent payments.

I had a lot of credit card debt and was using the credit cards for ten months after the accident until the settlement check arrived, so I was thankful to get out of debt with the settlement money. I also gave a huge amount away and was able to bless a number of people in various ways.

I must admit, I also wasted a lot of money on diamond jewelry after receiving the settlement check. I always loved marquise cut jewelry and purchased a marquise diamond that was over one carat and had it mounted in a beautiful setting. I called that ring my P&S ring, which stood for the pain and suffering that I endured because of the accident. Naturally, I received a lot of compliments regarding it and loved wearing it, at least for a season. I also purchased other expensive diamond jewelry. I enjoyed wearing some of the jewelry for a couple of years, even though they weren't worn often since I wasn't going away much. What a waste of money! I was able to sell the P&S ring at a great loss and the diamond studs, but still have a couple pieces to sell as of this writing. That jewelry means nothing to me now, and I'm thankful for God's mercy and forgiveness for that wasteful spending! It was a big lesson learned, and Holy Spirit changed me from the inside out regarding my spending habits, which have drastically changed. I'm very grateful for that change!

Chapter 10

Thoughts on Writing a Book

I've had occasional thoughts in the last several years about writing a book due to some of the out-of-the-ordinary experiences I've had with the Lord. I wanted to encourage others in their walk with the Lord and to trust and rely on Him to guide their steps and fulfill their destiny, but they were fleeting thoughts, here and gone. That is, until early in 2021, when the thoughts were stronger and didn't go away. Then on March 31, 2021, I was sharing with Matthew Hildebrand and Joel Hildebrand about some of my April 1 experiences and that I was looking forward to the next day since it was another April 1. Joel said, "You should write a book." I just stared at him speechless for a couple of seconds, thinking to myself, this is a confirmation to what I've been thinking, but didn't share that with him. His words were a great encouragement to me!

The following day was April 1, 2021, my forty-second anniversary with Jesus! I stayed home all day in my jammies and in the Word and prayer. While in prayer, I sensed **yes** on writing a book! This would be a totally new experience for me, but Holy Spirit wrote the whole Bible, so my trust was in Him to lead and guide me in the project. I exercised faith and started taking action steps by thinking and reviewing things that happened in my life, gathering information from journals, and asking Holy Spirit to bring things to my remembrance that He wants in the book.

Two other confirmations about writing a book include my granddaughter's boyfriend at the time saying on Easter, April 4, 2021, I should write a novel after I shared some things that happened in my life. A novel isn't what was on my heart, but it was still another person saying I should write a book. And then about a month later, I was talking with a neighbor about my seeds and seedlings for tomato and other vegetable plants when she asked if I had records of everything, and then said, "You should write a book." I know seeds and gardening have nothing to do with what I'm supposed to write about, but it was another person saying I should write a book! Perhaps I should rephrase that last sentence because, spiritually speaking, seeds and planting and reaping are an integral part of walking with the Lord!

The enemy has tried many times to put self-doubt and unbelief in my mind regarding writing a book, and I must admit I've given into these thoughts too often, but Holy Spirit brings me back to thinking on I am anointed and equipped to do this through Him, and not based on my own strengths or abilities.

Holy Spirit has woken me in the middle of the night a number of times when I sensed to go and write. I discovered this is a good time for me because I'm able to be more intentional and focused on writing, rather than being distracted by seeing things that should be attended to or hearing things outside that perk my interest. Except, there is a fire department right across the street where I live, so when their sirens go off, I always stop and pray for their safety and ask the Lord to help them accomplish whatever emergency they face. Then I check online to see where they are headed and for what purpose. At times, my sleep is often very sporadic and only for three to four hours at a time or less, but then at other times I'll have eight to nine hours or more with some good REM and deep sleep time, which is great. Knowing sleep is so important for our bodies, I've struggled in my mind at times with not having a good sleep schedule, but then accepted that if Holy Spirit woke me to write, then it is fine. I relate it to times when Holy Spirit wakes me to pray about something, or when I've scheduled times in the middle of the night to pray for mission teams on short-term assignments in other countries; it is Holy Spirit directing me so it will all work out regardless of how much sleep I get, and I am able to take naps during the day too.

Chapter 11

A Quick Overview of My April 1 Experiences

There are a lot more details of these experiences woven throughout the book but, I wanted to give a quick overview as well.

I often wondered why so many amazing things happened to me on April 1 throughout the years, so I was excited to learn in the spring of 2022 that from the middle of March to the middle of April is the first month of the year, called Nisan, in the ancient Hebraic calendar, which is a lunisolar calendar. The Lord spoke to Moses and Aaron about this in Exodus

12:1-2, **"The Lord said to Moses and Aaron in the land of Egypt, 'This month shall be to you the beginning of months, the first month of the year to you.'"**

The Lord made the month of Nisan the beginning of months, the first month of the year for the Jewish people, and is also known as Abib, which means spring or the beginning of the agricultural year for the Jewish people. So I think of it as a time of new beginnings; therefore, my April 1 experiences make so much sense since so many new things started happening on April 1 dates and some other significant things happened in the beginning of April for me. Things that happened later in March would have been a part of orchestrating my new beginning April 1 experiences too. I've had other amazing things happen at other times of the year too, but my April 1 experiences naturally stand out to me, and when February and March come, I start to look forward to April 1 with great anticipation and expectation! There are many things recorded in the Bible of things God did that were so significant in the month of Nisan as well.

Please don't misunderstand what I'm saying because God does amazing things every day of the year, not just on April 1, but for some reason that is the date He chose for many amazing things to happen in my life.

My quick overview follows.

April 1, 1974

Went to AA to quit drinking but did end up drinking that night. However, I went back the following night and quit drinking!

April 1, 1979

I asked Jesus to forgive my sins and come into my life, so I became a born-again, new creation in Christ! Three Scripture references to mention being born again or becoming a new creation follow.

Jesus answered him, "I assure you, most solemnly I tell you, that unless a person is born again (anew, from above), he cannot ever

see (know, be acquainted with, and experience) the kingdom of God." John 3:3

Therefore if any person is [ingrafted] in Christ (the Messiah) he is a new creation (a new creature altogether); the old [previous moral and spiritual condition] has passed away. Behold, the fresh and new has come! 2 Corinthians 5:17

For neither is circumcision [now] of any importance, nor uncircumcision, but [only] a new creation [the result of a new birth and a new nature in Christ Jesus, the Messiah]. Galatians 6:15

April 1, 2016

I had been praying, hoping the settlement checks from the accident on June 9, 2015, would come sooner, but they arrived at my attorney's office on April 1, 2016, and I went that very day and signed the one since it was made out to both my attorney's office and me. Then they mailed me a check for the full amount since I was paying for their services on an hourly basis as they were being rendered. The second check was mailed directly to Medicare, due to a required partial payback since there was an insurance settlement. I love the Lord's timing rather than mine giving another amazing April 1 to me!

April 1, 2019

On August 25, 2000, on my fifty-sixth birthday, I moved into a brand new, big, beautiful home the Lord provided for me to live in for almost nineteen years; April 1, 2019, was the final day of that being my address. It was also the first day I spent overnight at a friend's home waiting for Holy Spirit's guidance to know where I would be living next.

April 1, 2021

While in prayer, Holy Spirit confirmed that I was to write this book.

April 1, 2022

Holy Spirit spoke to me regarding some future things, which I'm not free to share at this time.

I love hearing doves cooing and seeing them and used to feed them down at the big house. I had only heard them from a distance since moving into the apartment—until March 31, 2022, when a single dove was sitting on my deck railing when I arrived home. I was excited to see it, and it didn't fly away right away, either. I immediately got my phone out and took a picture of it. At first, it was a single dove, but in a couple of days, a pair started visiting me regularly on the deck railing and even on the floor of the deck. At times, there were three of them together on the deck. They didn't always fly away when I got close to them, either. I would hear them cooing in the early morning and look outside to see them basking in the sun on the railing. This happened daily for weeks, then they would show up and land on my vehicle or in trees in my neighbor's yard occasionally when I was sitting outside. Then I would see one on the roof peak when I would come back from walking, but they haven't been around for a while. It was a special blessing to me, which I will continue to hold precious in my memory!

A dove always reminds me of when Jesus was baptized, and the Spirit of God descended from the heavens like a dove and rested on Him!

Chapter 12

A Few Other Unique Experiences

◇ President Ronald Reagan was shot on March 30, 1981. I went to the house at the church where prayer meetings were held, assuming a lot of people would be there to pray for President Reagan, but I was the only one there. I stayed there for a couple of hours, not sure exactly how long I was there. What I am sure of is that I was released to stop praying at the exact time the surgery was completed on him. I saw on a TV in another room when leaving that they just announced the surgery was over when I had stopped praying. We never know how Holy Spirit will use us when praying in tongues for situations!

◇ A Fear of Crossing Bridges: When I was a teenager, I used to go with a friend to a place her family had near a river, and we'd go swimming there off the end of a pier. One time some guys were with us, and one guy was holding me down under the water. I thought I was going to drown and naturally was very scared. He did let me go, and when I came to the surface, he was laughing and thought it was funny!

I'm sure that's where my fear of crossing bridges came from and for years, I didn't want to cross bridges and especially not the long ones, like on trips.

Early in my Christian walk, I registered for a singles conference and was driving by myself to the conference in Virginia Beach. I did not know I would be crossing a very long bridge. When I started driving on it, I began screaming at the enemy, taking authority over the spirit of fear of the water and of crossing bridges, and an immediate calm came over me. I was truly amazed at the peace I had crossing that long bridge, which included a section of a tunnel under the water too. When writing this section of the book, I checked to see how long the bridge is, and it is 79,200 feet, so that equals fifteen miles! I know I wouldn't have gone that route if I would have known that ahead of time, but I'm so glad I went that way and dealt with the fear! Thank You, Holy Spirit, for Your amazing help!

The conference was being held at the hotel I was also staying at and was right on the beach. I don't recall much of the conference content but do know that one night after one of the sessions, I was sitting outside thinking about the meeting when Holy Spirit told me to go step into the water. I felt a little hesitant at first because there were some other people outside too, but I got up and walked down to the water in the dark and took several steps into it. The session at the conference related to God calling us into deep waters with Him, and my stepping into the water was a sign of obedience and that I would follow Him and trust Him! Something inside of me changed that night in the water!

◊ Back in the 1980s, a group of singles from the church I was a member of went on a picnic at the Middle Creek Wildlife Management Area. We were having a great day when suddenly a woman fell to the ground with blood coming out of her nose and mouth and was unresponsive. A nurse was there and came to try to help the woman. I laid hands on the woman's legs and started confessing Ezekiel 16:6, over and over which reads, **"And when I passed by thee, and saw thee polluted in thine own blood, I said unto thee when thou wast in thy blood, Live; yes, I said unto thee when thou wast in thy blood, Live"** (KJV). The blood did stop flowing, and the ambulance came and took her to the hospital. After they left, the nurse told me she had never seen anything like what just happened, with the blood flow stopping like that, in all her nursing history. I shared with her that I heard a testimony on a 700 Club cassette tape series—cassette tape, words out of the past—where a woman was sharing about a time when she was in the hospital and had blood coming out of every pore of her body and the doctors couldn't stop it. A friend came to visit one day and kept reading this Scripture over her again and again and again until the blood stopped coming out of her, and she was healed!

We all found out later that the woman taken to the hospital died, which we naturally all felt bad about. It made me wonder what other Scripture I could have spoken that would have saved her life, but it sure showed me the power of speaking the Scripture too! And granted, this Scripture is talking about being in natal blood, but nonetheless it worked to stop the blood flowing!

I used this Scripture for a nosebleed my daughter had once when she was young, and her nose stopped bleeding too. I've shared this Scripture with other people who were dealing with issues of blood or knew of someone who was, but never received any feedback from them.

◊ A friend was very sick in the hospital, but the doctors couldn't do anything for her, so they sent her home. When I heard about it, I had such a stirring and strong sense in my spirit and knew I had to go to her. In my vehicle on the way to her home, I smelled a horrible smell and knew it was the smell of death!

Her husband took me to their bedroom upstairs as soon as I got there. Naturally, she wasn't in good shape at all, but when I tried to pray for her, I didn't have peace inside to pray, so I told them that and started asking questions to find out what was blocking me from praying.

Holy Spirit helped her identify an area where the enemy had her in bondage, and when she agreed to deal with it, Holy Spirit had me sing over her and tell her to rise and be healed. She rose off the deathbed and was totally healed. To God be the glory, for it was His doing!

This person shares her story with others and tells people that I raised her from her deathbed, but it wasn't me; it was Holy Spirit working through a human vessel. Neither one of us remembers the exact date this happened, but both believe it was in 1986.

◇ The company I was employed by did a lot of subcontract work for other large corporations. Back in the late 1980s, in one of the companies we were hired as subcontractors, I kept seeing flames (not actual flames but saw them in the spirit realm) every time I passed by a particular area. It happened on a consistent basis, so I knew I had to share it with our contact at the company. I had no idea how he would respond to what I shared, but I knew I had to share with him. He advised me he would check it out and thanked me for the information. When he got back to me, he advised me there were chemicals being used inside the little area that should not have been being used. This could have caused a fire, which could have been a major disaster! I was so thankful that Holy Spirit kept showing me this and gave me the courage to share it.

⋄ I hardly dated at all after becoming a Christian, but back in the early 1990s, I was seeing a guy who bought me so many beautiful things, including clothing, which I had never experienced before in a dating relationship in my whole life. One evening at a church service, he said he wanted to take me to the shore for the weekend. It sounded like fun and I assumed we would have separate rooms. I was going to go until Holy Spirit spoke during the church service that evening and said, "Don't go, you are headed for trouble!" When the service was over, I told him I couldn't go with him; he didn't like it and was upset.

We had a mutual friend, which is how I met him, and I took everything he bought me to her place to return to him and never regretted it!

◇ I was headed to see my friend Joyce, and it was pouring down rain so hard that I could hardly see. I yelled at it and commanded it to stop and immediately it became a fine mist! Wow, that is an experience I'll never forget! I tried this at other times after that experience, and it didn't work; I have seen times where the rain greatly slowed down, but nothing compared to going from a downpour to a fine mist!

◇ In 2003, I was in Ohio driving home from a conference when I kept seeing a rainbow out in front of me. As I got closer and closer, it looked like it ended on the road ahead of me, and it did—**I drove right through the end of a rainbow!** I wish I could have taken a photo as I was approaching it. It made me think of God's faithfulness! It was an awesome experience!

◊ In 2008 or 2011, I drove to the Philadelphia Airport for the first time by myself to get a couple very frilly scarves that I saw and loved when traveling to Florida but didn't purchase at that time. When I got to the airport and asked people how I could do this, I kept being told I couldn't go through the gate to get to the scarves, but I didn't give up. I kept asking people, requesting they talk to someone above them. I asked God for favor, continually thanking Him for favor inside and whispering it to myself the whole time I was waiting for the woman to return. It took a while, but finally someone came back and said they would send someone with me so I could purchase the scarves! Hallelujah! God's favor is amazing even in the little, insignificant things!

◊ There was a heavy downpour of rain on Route 30 close to the exit to Route 222 one day when I was driving home from work. I was in the passing lane traveling through large amounts of water on the road when all of a sudden, my vehicle hydroplaned. I felt it hit the concrete barrier beside me. I screamed and closed my eyes, and seconds later opened my eyes to see that my car was now three lanes to the right of where I was originally. I had to move one lane left so I didn't end up getting onto Route 222! I was raising a HALLELUJAH for a long time and thanking God for His angels protecting me and for the fact there were no other vehicles around me at the time! I checked my car when I got home for any damage from hitting the barrier, but there wasn't any! Perhaps an angel pushed me and that's what I felt! I usually always think of that experience whenever I'm at the same place and it's raining. I continue to be thankful for God's protection! In my daily confessions, I thank God that He has given His angels charge over me to keep and protect me and that no evil befalls me, and no plague comes nigh my dwelling per Psalm 91:9-11.

◇ On February 25, 2016, there was a tornado warning for my location. I could hear the wind howling from inside the house, so I opened the front door and went outside. The wind was getting even stronger. I don't know that I've ever heard such a loud sound of the wind before—it was kind of scary. I yelled and took authority over it and told it to pass by our area and not to damage any properties in our area! No, I don't have a problem yelling at storms even if people hear me. I don't think anyone was outside at the time, but if they were, it didn't matter to me. Sadly, I learned that a barn was destroyed by it several miles away, though.

◊ I've been touched by an angel several times, and it usually happens when I need to be awakened from sleep for different reasons. I feel my leg or my side being pushed to wake up. Once, I was awake most of the night and praying in the morning until I drifted off to sleep. An angel pushed me on the arm and pushed me sideways, so naturally I awoke! I just smile when this happens, since I know God's angels are with me! Hebrews 1:14, states, **"Are not the angels all ministering spirits (servants) sent out in the service [of God for the assistance] of those who are to inherit salvation?"** This has happened more frequently over the last couple of years, from 2020 to 2023.

◊ In early May 2021, I was having issues with high blood pressure when the diastolic number was over one hundred at times and often in the high nineties, which I know isn't good. I wasn't sleeping well, eating well, or taking my supplements during this time and believe my immune system wasn't where it should have been. This was also the time that a minor case of shingles appeared on my chin with some little clusters. I applied apple cider vinegar on my chin, but that didn't help, so I looked in my essential oils book. Bergamot, which I had, was the second oil listed in relation to shingles, so I started using that full strength on the clusters and they cleared up in several days. I was thankful there was very little burning and no pain like I experienced when I had shingles on my back and side about twenty years ago!

The high blood pressure bothered me some, but then I started having some heart pains and heaviness in my chest and found myself allowing my thoughts to think about my mom dying so young at twenty-nine with heart problems. I was thinking, what if I needed heart surgery or had a stroke? I was almost expecting something negative to happen. The enemy was really playing with my mind. But then thoughts came to me from a sermon I heard recently when Jesus said to the disciples in Mark 4:35, **"Let us go** over to the other side [of the lake]" and they got in the boat to go there. Then Mark 4:37-40, says:

And a furious storm of wind [of hurricane proportions] arose, and the waves kept beating into the boat, so that it was already becoming filled. But He [Himself] was in the stern [of the boat], asleep on the [leather] cushion, and they awoke Him and said to Him, Master, do You not care that we are perishing? And He arose and rebuked the wind and said to the sea, Hush now! Be still (muzzled)! And the wind ceased [sank to rest as if exhausted by its beating) and there was [immediately] a great calm (a perfect peacefulness). He said to them, Why are you so timid and fearful? How is it that you have no faith (no firmly relying trust)?

While in prayer, Holy Spirit reminded me of something He spoke to me several weeks before that had to do with something happening in the future. Then faith took over and the negative thoughts were gone! My blood pressure was still running high for a couple of days, but then one morning when I awoke,

I was just free and felt totally different from the week before. My blood pressure was back to what was normal for me that evening, and the discomfort in heart and chest was gone!

Oh, the power of our thoughts and words, and Holy Spirit's words to us!

Words from two songs were on my heart after being freed above:

1) I stand, I stand in awe of You, and

2) You are good, good, so good! They stayed on my heart, and I was singing them for days.

◇ I know financial planning organizations and financial planners advise to save money for retirement and other things, but I'm so glad my Father had a different plan for my life. I was, and still am, experiencing His providential care in my finances.

A recent example of that care that happened in 2022 follows. For a year or more, I was having a very hard time reading the Bible and other normal things because I needed new lenses in my glasses. I would go to Gateway Bible online, choose X-large print, enlarge the screen even more, and then put cotton balls on my nose under my glasses, which made it easier to read. It didn't look pretty, but it worked—there was also a crack in one of the lenses. A friend who was aware of the cracked lens texted me in the middle of June and asked if the reason I didn't get my glasses fixed was because of money and if I had checked what the price would be to get it fixed. I texted back and advised that she was correct about the money and that I had just called for a price back in April for new lenses. I presented that need to my Father and thanked Him for His provision. The very next day, she texted back that she sensed she was to give me $300 toward that need, but when I received her check, it was for the full amount of the cost of the lenses! I was praising and thanking my Father and thanking my friend as well!

Chapter 13

Disappointments

Disappointed in God

I've had a lot of amazing experiences with God, but I've also had times of great disappointments involving the loss of people whose ages ranged from early thirties to early fifties that I prayed for and were not healed. Three of those people were very special friends who are now in Heaven with Jesus, and I look forward to being reunited with them in God's perfect timing. I was with the one person when she left this earth, and it hurt deeply, but I was also so glad she was now free from pain and enjoying the presence of Jesus. I know she is still laughing and making others laugh too. She helped so many people and was loved by so many, so I know I'm only one among many who experienced a great loss when she left us.

Disappointed in Others

Back in the nineties, I was hurt deeply and rejected by people who I respected, looked up to, valued their help and guidance in my walk with the Lord, and loved. Satan tried to use this to make me question God's love for me; but God taught me a big lesson through what happened with them, and that is that my emotional dependence, strength, energy, and validation must come from Him, and not from dependence on others! Yes, we can have good, strong relationships, but God wants to be our Source for all things and to rely on and trust in Him. People will fail us, but God won't. Yes, I have forgiven those who hurt and rejected me, but my trust in people was affected.

Disappointed in Myself

I've had a lot of disappointments in myself over things I've done or didn't do, and said or didn't say, since becoming a Christian, which are woven throughout this book with the biggest ones being:

◇ I didn't know how to be a mother to my daughter since I didn't have one growing up due to my mother dying at age twenty-nine when I was six, nor did I have a model of one in my life. More about this is shared in Chapter 7 under the heading Life Changing and Saving Prophetic Ministry Class Assignment. My daughter turned out amazing, in spite of me. She had a very traumatic experience in her life too that helped propelled her to become the person she is today and is helping so many other people in so many ways. I am so thankful she has returned to the Lord too! She is an entrepreneur running two businesses; one is a gym focusing on boxing conditioning, which she built into a community where people feel more like a family when they are there rather than just stopping for an hour at the gym. God is using her gym, EnVision Train Fitness, to minister to people in various ways outside of the physical training that happens, which she knows through texts or other messages people send her. I am so proud of her!

I'm also very thankful that my daughter and I have a wonderful relationship now!

She is a great mother too, raising a daughter, Allyssa Cox, who also has her own successful business. I am so proud of her as well!

I know single parenting isn't easy, but I encourage all single moms, and dads too for that matter, not to make your job your life and neglect your children, even if the job is in a Christian ministry! Due to my personality and being so focused on my work, I missed so much with my daughter growing up. Ask Holy Spirit to make a way for you to spend more time with your children!

◇ I regret the many years I spent focusing on myself and spending money foolishly and, yes, going into debt too, to try and make myself look good and feel good on the inside and outside, and especially all the money I wasted on jewelry after receiving the settlement check from the accident that resulted in both tibia bones being fractured in 2015. I gave away a very large amount out of that settlement money too, but that doesn't negate the money I wasted. I'm so thankful the blood of Jesus forgives wasteful spending sins too!

I am so thankful that I have been set free and have total peace with who I am and don't have to compare myself to others in any way. I don't have to explain myself to others for things I do that don't make sense to them either; some of the things I do don't make sense to me at the time either, but then with hindsight they do make sense later. My value and worth come from the Lord! I am fearfully and wonderfully made by Him to fulfill the destiny He planned for me!

I've made many mistakes along the way, but I always repented and received forgiveness and moved forward. My confidence is in Philippians 1:6:

And I am convinced and sure of this very thing, that He Who began a good work in you will continue until the day of Jesus Christ [right up to the time of His return], developing [that good work] and perfecting and bringing it to full completion in you.

We all experience disappointments in life, but I'm so thankful for a Scripture Holy Spirit has taken me to different times over the years regarding disappointments. Psalm 48 is a song about the greatness of God and a song of praise to Him and vs. 13 reads, **"Consider well her ramparts, go through her palaces and citadels, that you may tell the next generation [and cease recalling disappointments]."** Occasionally, I need to be reminded of those last four words—and cease recalling disappointments.

Chapter 14

BETH~EL:
House of God,
House of Prayer

Back in the early 1990s, I had a widow friend who was in her nineties. I visited her on a regular basis and often put her and her wheelchair in my vehicle, sometimes just to go for a ride to get her out of the house or visit a particular place. She lived with her daughter and son-in-law, which was a great blessing to her. They both had full-time jobs, so she was alone most of the time during the day. We both looked forward to the visits and became very good friends. I loved spending time with her and think of her from time to time and those thoughts still bring a smile to my face and a loving feeling in my heart!

Holy Spirit started connecting me to other, mostly older, widows on an individual basis, and the thought arose inside of me to get the widows together to do things as a group, and to invite other widows to join us. Several of them no longer drove a vehicle, so it was a way to get them out of the house and around other women who they could easily relate to. Some of the things we did include going to the park for a picnic lunch, eating together at restaurants or one of the widow's homes that was large enough for all of us to fit in easily, and attending a show at Sight & Sound Theatres. We also ate at a restaurant in Harrisburg and then went to see and hear the Brooklyn Tabernacle Choir at The Forum in November 1993. There was an average of ten of us, and we always had a wonderful time together. The widows would not pay for anything; God always provided the funds needed.

My brother greatly blessed one of the widows too. He was in the produce business, and when I found out one of the widows who lived alone didn't have money for fresh fruits and vegetables and told him about it, he said I could gather some food together after market was over and take to her at times. She loved getting the food, and it filled my heart with joy to see her so full of joy! My brother blessed the widows in other ways too.

We also had prayer times together, sharing needs and praying for each other and other situations and sharing Scriptures. The vision for Beth~El arose in my heart out of these times together. I saw a large home with several bedrooms with attached baths for individual women if someone wanted to live there or come and stay for a while, and then a large living room, dining room, and kitchen where women could gather for fellowship, prayer, Bible study, and so forth. Beth~El would be available for all widows to come and share in the community there, and naturally, for times of prayer.

We continued getting together for a season, until some of the widows were having physical problems and some went to their heavenly homes, so the group meetings stopped and the vision for Beth~El was put on the back burner, so to speak.

Renewed Vision & Focus

Over twenty years later, in December 2016, during a time of praying and reading the Word, the vision of Beth~El was on my heart and mind again. However, now I saw it as a place for women going through rough times who needed a place to stay for a while, to get away from the world and reconnect with God, to have time for prayer and Bible study, and to just forget what is going on in the outside world. It would be a place where women could be revived and refreshed.

On March 26, 2017, I was reading in the Psalms and was going to stop but sensed to continue reading. The words at the end of Psalm 118:5 spoke to me, **"Out of my distress I called upon the Lord; the Lord answered me and set me free and in a large place."** At this time, I would have still been dealing with mobility issues due to the accident and both tibia bones being fractured, but the end of the verse about being free and in a large place is what spoke to my heart since my dream for Beth~El is a "large" place! Large in the Hebrew means enlargement and is from a primitive root meaning to broaden, make room, make open wide!

I was also reminded that several times in the past, Isaiah 54:2 had been given to me, **"Enlarge the place of your tent, and let the curtains of your habitations be stretched out; spare not, lengthen your cords and strengthen your stakes."** Enlarge here means the same as in Psalm 118:5, mentioned in the previous paragraph. Tent means dwelling place, home, so naturally, I always think of my dream of Beth~El when reading this Scripture.

Then in the fall of 2021, the vision for Beth~El in relation to widows was on my heart again, but who's to say that God won't use Beth~El as a place for both to come and have fellowship and be refreshed and revived!

Holy Spirit has taken me to Habakkuk 2:3, a few times over the last several years, which is a great encouragement to me to keep believing and trusting in His timing for Beth~El! It reads:

For the vision is yet for an appointed time and it hastens to the end [fulfillment]; it will not deceive or disappoint. Though it tarry, wait [earnestly] for it, because it will surely come. It will not be behindhand on its appointed day.

Scripture References for BETH~EL

In Genesis 28, Isaac told his son, Jacob, to go to Padan-aram to take a wife from there, and not to take a wife of the daughters of Canaan. The sun was setting, so Jacob took a stone to put under his head and went to sleep—have to say it, I can't imagine sleeping with my head on a stone! Jacob had a dream in which the Lord spoke to him about his future, and when Jacob awoke, he said, **"Surely the Lord is in this place, and I did not know it."** He said it was the house of God and proceeded to use the stone he had put under his head to set up a monument to the vision in his dream. He poured oil on it, and he named the place Bethel, the house of God.

House of prayer is mentioned in the Old and New Testaments:

All these I will bring to My holy mountain

and make them joyful in My house of prayer. Their burnt offerings and their sacrifices will be accepted on My altar; for My house will be called a house of prayer for all peoples. Isaiah 56:7

And Jesus went into the temple (whole temple enclosure) and drove out all who bought and sold in the sacred place, and He turned over the four-footed tables of the money changers and the chairs of those who sold doves. He said to them, The Scripture says, My house shall be called a house of prayer; but you have made it a den of robbers. Matthew 21:12-13

One of my prayers when praying for widows is that they would know that their heavenly Husband has a plan for their lives and that He gives them a sense of purpose and vision. I believe for some, especially the older widows, that Beth~El could help give them that sense of purpose and to have the sense of community and enjoy being around other widows.

I greatly look forward to seeing how Father

is going to orchestrate the realization of Beth~El in the natural realm!

Chapter 15

God Has a Plan for Each of Our Lives

The following Scriptures have been the foundation for my walk of faith and trust in God's Providence to bring about His plans for my life. I hope they help you trust Him as well!

Lean on, trust in, and be confident in the Lord with all your heart and mind and do not rely on your own insight or understanding. In all your ways know, recognize, and acknowledge Him, and He will direct and make straight and plain your paths. Proverbs 3:5–6

The word "paths" here means a road, a highway, to travel.

Roll your works upon the Lord [commit and trust them wholly to Him; He will cause your thoughts to become agreeable to His will, and] so shall your plans be established and succeed. Proverbs 16:3

The word "works" here means an action, a product, property, occupation, thing offered, possessions, and more. I have shared this Scripture over and over with people who were seeking to know God's will about something. As we commit, or roll our works upon Him, He will cause our thoughts to become agreeable to His will, and so shall our plans be established and succeed! This is one of my favorite Scriptures.

For I know the thoughts and plans that I have for you, says the Lord, thoughts and plans for welfare and peace and not for evil, to give you hope in your final outcome. Jeremiah 29:11

Do not be conformed to this world (this

age), [fashioned after and adapted to its external, superficial customs], but be transformed (changed) by the [entire] renewal of your mind [by its new ideals and its new attitude], so that you may prove [for yourselves] what is the good and acceptable and perfect will of God, even the thing which is good and acceptable and perfect [in His sight for you]. Romans 12:2

For we are God's [own] handiwork (His workmanship), recreated in Christ Jesus, [born anew] that we may do those good works which God predestined (planned beforehand) for us [taking paths which He prepared ahead of time], that we should walk in them [living the good life which He prearranged and made ready for us to live]. Ephesians 2:10

[Not in your own strength] for it is God Who is all the while effectually at work in you [energizing and creating in you the power and desire], both to will and to work for His good pleasure and satisfaction and delight. Philippians 2:13

The above Scriptures leave no room for doubt that God has a specific plan for each of our lives, a destiny for each of us to fulfil! We do not come up with a plan for our lives and ask God to bless it, but seek His will for our lives and He will bring it to pass for His glory and honor! Jesus is our example to follow.

We are assured and know that [God being a partner in their labor] all things work together and are [fitting into a plan] for good to and for those who love God and are called according to [His] design and purpose.

For those whom He foreknew [of whom He was aware and loved beforehand], He also destined from the beginning [foreordaining them] to be molded into the image of His Son [and share inwardly His likeness], that He might become the firstborn among many brethren. Romans 8:28–29

Scriptures to Meditate on Regarding God's Faithfulness

But as for me, my prayer is to You, O Lord.

At an acceptable and opportune time, O God, in the multitude of Your mercy and the abundance of Your loving-kindness hear me, and in the truth and faithfulness of Your salvation answer me. Psalm 69:13

It is a good and delightful thing to give thanks to the Lord, to sing praises [with musical accompaniment] to Your name, O Most High, To show forth Your loving-kindness in the morning and Your faithfulness by night, With an instrument of ten strings and with the lute, with a solemn sound upon the lyre. For You, O Lord, have made me glad by Your works; at the deeds of Your hands I joyfully sing. How great are Your doings, O Lord! Your thoughts are very deep. Psalm 92:1–5

For the Lord is good; His mercy and loving-kindness are everlasting, His faithfulness and truth endure to all generations. Psalm 100:5

Not to us, O Lord, not to us but to Your

name give glory, for Your mercy and loving-kindness and for the sake of Your truth and faithfulness! Psalm 115:1

Hear my prayer, O Lord, give ear to my supplications! In Your faithfulness answer me, and in Your righteousness. Psalm 143:1

O Lord, You are my God; I will exalt You, I will praise Your name, for You have done wonderful things, even purposes planned of old [and fulfilled] in faithfulness and truth. Isaiah 25:1

It is because of the Lord's mercy and loving-kindness that we are not consumed, because His [tender] compassions fail not. They are new every morning; great and abundant is Your stability and faithfulness. The Lord is my portion or share, says my living being (my inner self); therefore will I hope in Him and wait expectantly for Him. The Lord is good to those who wait hopefully and expectantly for Him, to those who seek Him [inquire of and for Him and require Him by right of necessity and on the authority of God's word]. Lamentations 3:22–25

God is faithful (reliable, trustworthy, and therefore ever true to His promise, and He can be depended on); by Him you were called into companionship and participation with His Son, Jesus Christ our Lord. 1 Corinthians 1:9

Faithful is He Who is calling you [to Himself] and utterly trustworthy, and He will also do it [fulfill His call by hallowing and keeping you]. 1 Thessalonians 5:24

Yet the Lord is faithful, and He will strengthen [you] and set you on a firm foundation and guard you from the evil [one]. 2 Thessalonians 3:3

If we are faithless [do not believe and are untrue to Him], He remains true (faithful to His Word and His righteous character), for He cannot deny Himself. 2 Timothy 2:13

Chapter 16

What Does the Future Hold?

In one respect, it would be nice to know what all the future holds, but that would not require faith and be pleasing to God, which requires faith in accordance with Hebrews 11:6:

But without faith it is impossible to please and be satisfactory to Him. For whoever would come near to God must [necessarily] believe that God exists and that He is the rewarder of those who earnestly and diligently seek Him [out].

Plus, walking in faith enables us to grow in our relationship with the Lord and learn to know Him more deeply and intimately, as Paul states in Philippians 3:10:

[For my determined purpose is] that I may know Him [that I may progressively become more deeply and intimately acquainted with Him, perceiving and recognizing and understanding the wonders of His Person more strongly and more clearly], and that I may in that same way come to know the power outflowing from His resurrection [which it exerts over believers], and that I may so share His sufferings as to be continually transformed [in spirit into His likeness even] to His death, [in the hope]

Now faith is the assurance (the confirmation, the title deed) of the things [we] hope for, being the proof of things [we] do not see and the conviction of their reality [faith perceiving as real fact what is not revealed to the senses]. Hebrews 11:1

Walking in faith, not knowing ahead of time what is going to happen, is much more exciting, and scary at times too, but so worth it to be able to look back and see how God has planned ahead of time for our steps and Holy Spirit guides and directs us accordingly.

Using faith, I do look forward to Beth~El becoming a reality and sharing with widows and others as Holy Spirit directs. (See Chapter 14 for more information on Beth~El.) Currently, there are thirteen widows that I pray for daily by name and have individual connections and times together with several of them. I'm sure that number will increase too. I also pray for what I call all of God's widow wives, since He is their Husband now.

My calling is prayer, so I know praying will always be a big part of my life. I love praying in tongues and seeking God's heart to know what to pray about. At times, I have no idea what I'm praying about, but trust and know Holy Spirit is using my prayers. Other times, Holy Spirit puts people and/or situations on my heart to pray about, and often has me reach out to people and let them know they are on God's heart and ask if there is something I can be praying for them about or share what Holy Spirit has put on my heart in relation to them. I look forward to more supernatural happenings through prayer for God's glory and honor!

My Father's thoughts and ways are so much higher than mine, and He knows the plans He has for me, so I always want Holy Spirit directing my thoughts and steps into my Father's will since He can do infinitely beyond my highest prayers, desires, thoughts, hopes, or dreams in accordance with another one of my favorite Scriptures, Ephesians 3:20:

Now to Him Who, by (in consequence of) the [action of His] power that is at work within us, is able to [carry out His purpose and] do superabundantly, far over and above all that we [dare] ask or think [infinitely beyond our highest prayers, desires, thoughts, hopes, or dreams]—

Was I always faithful? No, but my Father always remained faithful, even at times when it didn't look like it in the natural realm! Thankfully, in accordance with 2 Timothy 2:13, His faithfulness isn't based on mine, **"If we are faithless [do not believe and**

are untrue to Him], He remains true (faithful to His Word and His righteous character), for He cannot deny Himself."

I sincerely hope reading about God's faithfulness and the things He has done in and through my life increases your faith and trust in Him, and that you are able to do what Colossians 1:4 says so that others will hear of the faithfulness of God in your lives, **"For we have heard of your faith in Christ Jesus [the leaning of your entire human personality on Him in absolute trust and confidence in His power, wisdom, and goodness]..."**

If you haven't accepted Jesus as your Savior, I encourage you to do that right now. Simply ask Jesus to forgive your sins and come into your heart. Then thank God for forgiving your sins. By saying these words, you will be born again spiritually and receive the free gift of salvation, be reconciled back to God, and spend eternity in heaven. Holy Spirit will help you on your journey here on the earth too.

Read the Bible, starting with the gospel of

John in the New Testament and get involved in a Bible-believing church and allow the Words of the Bible and Holy Spirit to transform you into the person who your Heavenly Father already sees you as.

If you accepted Jesus in the past but walked away from following and trusting in Him, repent, receive forgiveness, and be reconciled back to God!

~ He is Trustworthy and Faithful ~
~ He's Directing My Steps ~
~ He'll Direct Your Steps Too ~
~ Trust Him ~

REFERENCES

1   Roberts, Oral. 1977. *The Daily Guide to Miracles*.

2   Sandford, John, and Paula Sandford. 1982. The Transformation of the Inner Man. South Plainfield, NJ: Bridge Pub.

3   Smith Wigglesworth. 2020. Ever Increasing Faith. S.L.: Bibliotech Press.

4   Evans, Tony. 2019. The Power of Jesus' Names. Harvest House Publishers.

Printed in the USA
CPSIA information can be obtained
at www.ICGtesting.com
CBHW031208211023
1440CB00004B/12